T0361202

Do More with Less

In current, uncertain times, it is important for businesses, whether private, public or third sector, to prepare for unexpected impacts. This book offers a way forward that brings individuals and their employers together to deliver a future that is ready to take advantage of opportunities, be ready for threats, "do sustainability" and save money at the same time.

Do More with Less takes conventional improvement techniques and suggests new ways to deploy them to improve both Efficiency and Effectiveness of organisations. The proposed programme is cost-neutral since it can be paid out of the improvements in effectiveness and efficiency: wasted time, effort, materials and budget. At a strategic level, this book introduces a key performance indicator linking resource use to corporate effectiveness, thereby bringing together sustainability, business success and waste reduction. The contents then cover the entire improvement process from initial audit through to implementing the improvements together with useful suggestions on ways to maintain the success and to control the gains. Techniques such as problem spotting and developing real-world solutions are presented as well as the necessary communications and marketing tools to support the improvement process.

This book is aimed at individuals who want to make a difference at work personally and at organisations that want to be successful in difficult and uncertain times. It presents ideas and techniques that are easy to learn, simple to carry out and practical to everyone.

Uly Ma is an experienced and motivating consultant with more than 20 years of experience in operational process effectiveness. Following his doctorate research, Uly worked as a metallurgist in product development. He worked for the UK government's energy efficiency programme in the 1990s and has since been providing process improvement and sustainability advice to both the private and public sector. His project NoWaste®, utilised during the London Olympics construction, is now part of the London 2012 Learning Legacy.

Do More with Less

A Guide for Uncertain Times

Uly Ma

Routledge
Taylor & Francis Group

LONDON AND NEW YORK

First published 2018
by Routledge
2 Park Square, Milton Park, Abingdon, Oxon OX14 4RN

and by Routledge
711 Third Avenue, New York, NY 10017

Routledge is an imprint of the Taylor & Francis Group, an informa business

© 2018 Uly Ma

British Library Cataloguing-in-Publication Data
A catalogue record for this book is available from the British Library

Library of Congress Cataloging-in-Publication Data
A catalog record for this book has been requested

ISBN: 9781138217041 (hbk)
ISBN: 9781138217058 (pbk)
ISBN: 9781315441641 (ebk)

Typeset in Bembo
by codeMantra

This book is dedicated to my wife Karen, without whom nothing would have got done.

Contents

Figures and tables

Figures

Tables

Acknowledgements

Just like any significant undertaking, getting there requires input from people. This book is in your hands only because of lots of people giving me encouragement, support, criticism (constructive or otherwise), ideas, knowledge and food. The support has been generous and automatic, no sooner than I mentioned I was writing another book than the response came: "What? Another book? How can we help?"

First, without my wife Karen, the task would have been much, much harder – thank you.

I would like to thank my former publisher, Jonathan Norman, who is now managing the Knowledge Hub, for his encouragement and willingness towards another book from me.

Big thanks to Claudine Blamey of the Crown Estate, Edward Dixon of Land Securities, my accountant Ellen English, Adam Foley of the ACCA, Greg Chant-Hall of Skanska, Sij Dhanju of Arcadis (UK) Catherine Garbi of garbimatcham architects, Jeremy Keeley of Keeley Carlisle, Louise Kingham OBE of the Energy Institute, Andrew Kinsey of MACE, Zoe Le Grand of Forum for the Future, Assad Maqbool of Trowers & Hamlins LLP, Colin Middleton of Tower Hamlets Council, Linda Richards of Databac and Deltcho and George Vitchev of Renaissance Finance International.

I also want to thank my students at London South Bank University for their enthusiasm when I bounced some of my ideas off them, as well as for their vague promises to buy this book. My colleagues at LSBU: Colston Sanger, Thor Ingvarsson and Bing Shi who listened to my ideas and offered suggestions for improvement.

A special group of long-time colleagues provided ideas, content and opportunities to debate various topics. Thanks to: Anastasia Marinopoulou of Progress Through, Peter Willmott of SA Partners, Isabelle Beaumont of Workplace Futures and Rebecca Lovelace of Circle Three Consulting.

Special thanks to the Worshipful Company of Constructors who gave me encouragement when I presented ideas that led to this book.

Introduction

What do Niels Bohr, noted scientist, and Viktor Chernomyrdin, former Russian prime minister, have in common?

Both were quoted as saying that prediction, or forecasting, is very difficult, especially about the future.[1]

Nevertheless, the world as we know it is likely to become more uncertain: When I started writing this book in spring 2016, the UK was a grumbling European Union (EU) member state, the USA was in the throes of an election campaign, France and Germany were on track for their respective elections in 2017 and concerns for businesses included whether the Federal Reserve would raise its prime rate and whether China's debt would get even higher.

Looking forward to spring 2017, the UK, still a grumbling member state, is leaving the EU, and it is getting a third national ballot in two years, the USA has a somewhat unpredictable president, France's election (as I write) is in a cliff hanger first round and the future of Germany's long-serving chancellor looks less secure. On top of that, there is tension in Europe, Asia, Africa, South America and the Middle East. Protectionism and populist governments appear to be ascendant. One thing is certain – the future seems to promise a lot of uncertainty.

What's next? Is there a best way forward for businesses in this time of uncertainty?

Besides the new uncertainties, some old certainties are still around: customer expectations of lower prices; society demands for better accountability from businesses and government;[2] investors clamouring for higher returns; and a general acceptance that sustainability is a component part of every business, albeit generally as a cost centre. However, I will suggest that instead of doom and gloom, it is more like the opening paragraph of Charles Dickens' *A Tale of Two Cites*: "It was the best of times, it was the worst of times…"

Sure, in the short term, we appear to be looking into the abyss: We, in the UK, will need to pay phone roaming charges after the UK leaves Europe! More seriously, if something goes wrong in the Korean Peninsula, it will be a wholesale abyss for lots of people. Nonetheless, I believe that the uncertainty also offers an opportunity for us to rethink the way we do things and get ahead of the competition.

Instead of waiting for something to happen and give us a sign of the way ahead, we can create our own way ahead by creating a stronger organisation. We can do something that preserves jobs, reduces our costs, raises our skills, innovates more and enhances our competitiveness. I call this Everyday Sustainability.

Everyday Sustainability comes from the sustainability that is often in the press or media. It has similar elements, like respecting people and respecting the environment, but is more focussed on what the individual can do in a practical, simple and easy way every day. It is not about fancy tree-loving rhetoric or eye-popping new technologies, but instead it is about getting down to exploring what we do and how we work, and aiming to do better.

No, it is not snake oil or the Holy Grail, but it is an achievable strategy for businesses and will make our organisations (more) ready for an uncertain future. This is not just for the UK alone; every country and organisation can benefit from this. It is also not just for private companies; this is equally applicable to public sector organisations and companies in the non-profit sectors too. And before you ask, no, it is not about being greener either.

This book is aimed at individuals and teams in businesses who want to get ahead and stay ahead in uncertain times. You may be a manager, an executive, an engineer, a worker or even an investor; this book is for you.

You can use this book to help you improve the way your organisation works, to strengthen its capabilities in uncertain times, to explore details about operational improvements, to look at ways to cut waste and to assess whether your investments are with an organisation that is well managed, therefore, giving you a better chance of good returns.

In this book, I bring together Uncertainty and Everyday Sustainability as a cause and a solution, respectively. This book is therefore about how businesses become ready to take advantage of opportunities and to deal with threats in an age of uncertainty. It is about delivering more when budgets are tight, when laws are getting more complex, when customers are becoming more demanding and when our future looks uncertain. It is about paying attention, not just to what we do, but also to how we do it. It is about engaging our people into good business practices and getting the most from our technology investments. It is about recovering cash currently lost in the business through waste, and it is about better overall use of resources. It is about Doing More with Less.

Structure of this book

This book has three sections: background, doing Everyday Sustainability and keeping it going. These are described below.

Chapters 1 to 3 provide the background to Everyday Sustainability, outline the basic principles and describe how this relates to other sustainability themes like energy use and climate change.

Chapter 1 sets the scene for Uncertainty and explores a time line of our conception of sustainability and how we get from climate change and energy efficiency to Everyday Sustainability.

Chapter 2 introduces Energy Productivity, the Key Performance Indicator (KPI) of Everyday Sustainability. The usefulness of this KPI is discussed as well as how it can be used as an indicator of your organisation's performance, why it is useful for investors and lenders and why you should deploy it in your organisation.

Chapter 3 describes the three components of Everyday Sustainability: Technology and Capabilities, People and Behaviour and Managing Processes, and how these form a stable foundation in uncertain times.

Chapters 4 to 6 turn the focus onto our organisation and how we carry out our daily work, finding out about known and hidden problems and how to deal with them.

Chapter 4 is about the way we work. It explores the way we gather information and make decisions. This chapter introduces Value Adding, Value Enabling and Waste in terms of business processes and everyday procedures. It also discusses how we use technology and whether we need to go for the most cutting edge kit.

Chapter 5 gets down to auditing our processes and procedures to get an idea of our Energy Productivity. It introduces the two forms of energy use at work: Operational Energy and Systems Energy and the relationship between everyday activities and how these add, enable or subtract value. This chapter also looks at the Facilities Management team, which often comprises a diverse collection of subcontractors, and how they can help us identify problems at work.

Chapter 6 gets deeper into process analysis and looking at the various tools and techniques that can help us identify and analyse value and waste at work.

Chapter 7 is about implementing solutions and improving the way we work. Again, there are tools and techniques that can help, but the focus is on Everyday Sustainability, which means whatever improvements we make, they should be sustainable. In other words, we should not have to revisit the same problem year after year.

Chapter 8 is called The Boss' Action Plan. It is the high-level view of how to start an Everyday Sustainability initiative: how to move your organisation from the Current State to the Future State. For those of us who are not the boss (yet), this chapter also includes tips on how to persuade your boss through addressing the critical issues in your proposal.

Chapters 9 and 10 are about communicating the message of Everyday Sustainability as a tonic to Uncertainty and to get the improvements embedded into the organisation's fabric.

Chapter 9 is about how to sell the Everyday Sustainability message and how to encourage take up. This chapter also looks at communications and the dissemination of ideas together with how active persuasion can help change behaviour.

Chapter 10 is about keeping the initiative going. It introduces the support activities that support the corporate strategy. This chapter also looks at rewarding the employees as well as supporting society with practical everyday activities.

Appendix 1 describes the Energy Productivity KPI framework in greater detail through the Overall Effectiveness technique.

Appendix 2 is different to most other back-of-the-book stuff (i.e. usually boring). This is a primer for those who are not familiar with management techniques, Lean or Six Sigma jargon and other delights that do not necessarily fit into the flow of the book but are often quite interesting. This section, therefore, acts as an extended glossary of the various tools, techniques and jargon described in the book and my efforts of translating these into plain(er) English. It also includes a somewhat nerdy (but fun) discussion on the limitations of a well-known risk management tool: Failure Modes and Effects Analysis (FMEA).

With all these goodies, you certainly should not miss Appendix 2. In fact, don't be conventional – read Appendix 2 first!

Appendix 3 introduces a tool to help develop new policies and actions to deal with uncertainty and changes.

Using the tools and techniques

I describe and list a wide range of tools and techniques in this book. Some of you may find that I suggest their use in unconventional situations, like using a marketing tool for communications planning or a design tool to develop policy, or use Lean/Six Sigma tools for just about everything.

This is because I see tools and techniques as what they are, titles notwithstanding. You have probably used a screwdriver to tighten screws, to lever off the top of a can of paint, to wedge open a door and perhaps to chip some paint off a door you painted. Movies have shown us that duct tape can save the day in just about any situation. So let's have no hang-ups about what the tools and techniques are called or classified. Use them to help you – as long as they are appropriate and actually get the job done.

And consider some of them to be checklists – they are there to remind you of things that may have slipped your mind.

Although health and safety at work can be seen as part of Everyday Sustainability, it is legislated differently in different jurisdictions, and there are regular updates to the legislation. My discussions on this area are mostly implied – do a risk assessment as part of any improvement action, and if you're not sure, ask someone and then do another risk assessment. You must act to mitigate or minimise any risk by redesigning the action if necessary.

Transport is an area not covered by this book. With the incoming technologies of self-driving and electric vehicles, as well as artificial intelligence control systems (and all the likely legislation), there is too much speculation on what could be possible in logistics, distribution and blue sky algorithms.

When standards and legislation are agreed, then it will be time to explore transport and how it can contribute to Everyday Sustainability.

Finally, you don't need a degree in rocket science to make this book work for you (I don't have one either). Yes, it does include many tools and techniques as well as lots of diagrams, but I intend these to be simple to use, easy to understand and practical to your work.

Notes

1 Attributed to Bohr: "Prediction is very difficult. Especially about the future." and attributed to Chernomyrdin: "Forecasting is a complicated thing, especially when it comes to forecasting the future." – Chernomyrdin was famous for saying rather convoluted things.
2 Actually, "society" demands more accountability from just about everyone, except itself.

1 Uncertainty, sustainability and waste

To start, let's define a few terms I will be using throughout this book.

Uncertainty means situations where we are not sure of the outcome or things that are not known to us.

Sustainability, in a strict definition, means keeping things going. However, conventionally it can mean a whole host of things: using the right amount of resources to do the required job, protect the environment, plant trees, not print your emails and save the polar bears.

Everyday Sustainability is a term I coined to describe the activities we can do (every day) to keep our organisations going, to protect the environment through using the right amount of resources and to, well, save money from reducing waste – which both keep the organisation going and use the optimal amount of resources. The important thing about "doing Everyday Sustainability" is that it needs to be simple to do, easy to learn and practical enough to make sense to everyone.

Now, you may think I am going to have a hard time joining these themes into a rational and logical discussion, but no, it is not (too) difficult to bring these together. They join up because uncertainty means what were constants before are no longer there, and this can blow a hole in our sustainability plans. People then tend to overreact to uncertainty and throw money (and resources) at the problem and therefore blow another hole in sustainability. Then we suddenly realise that in conventional businesses, the sustainability function is a cost centre. Oops, another hole and the good ship, sustainability, is rapidly sinking in the sea of uncertainty.[1]

One way to deal with uncertainty is to take a fresh look at our world, our organisations and our activities – to see whether our existing concepts and approaches will work in the new and ever-changing environment. I therefore suggest we need to reassess our outlook and update our thinking to see every uncertainty as a possible opportunity.

So far, in 2017, every week brings news of some change in laws, in geopolitics and in business deals, and each of these changes comes with its own accompanying uncertainty. Uncertainty can mean a lot of things: unknown directions for our organisations and, with them, unknown opportunities and unknown risk, as shown in Figure 1.1.

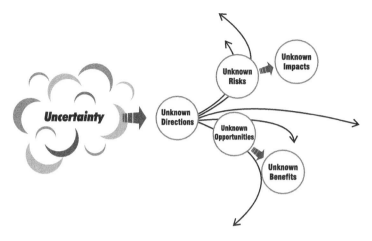

Figure 1.1 Uncertainty.

But if you look beyond the headlines, then every opportunity will offer unknown benefits and every risk will offer unknown impacts. I would like to think that with a bit of effort, we can make sure we are ready – ready to take advantage of opportunities coming our way and equally ready to deal with risks in whatever direction our organisation takes. To do that, I suggest we make sure our people are ready to respond competently and in an appropriate way; our processes are robust, running efficiently and effectively; and we, as an organisation, can make the most from the technologies we deploy.

These three factors, I believe, make up Everyday Sustainability. This is sustainability both in its classical sense of continuing as well as the modern sense of using resources properly, as shown in Figure 1.2.

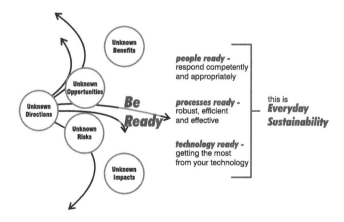

Figure 1.2 Everyday Sustainability.

However, before we start exploring Everyday Sustainability, we need to see how uncertainty affects our thinking about global economics and climate and how uncertainty shapes the world's evolving actions on sustainability. To look at how uncertainty shaped the way we think and act, let's examine one of the best everyday examples about uncertainty: our weather!

Bad weather

Daily weather forecasts show you a percentage likelihood of rain. In a place the size of London (around 1570 km^2 or about 600 square miles), a 10 per cent chance of rain at 11:30 can mean 100 per cent in your part of London and no rain in other areas – see, weather is uncertain! To deal with that uncertainty means being ready: we carry umbrellas, raincoats or hats, or we get wet. Those of us of a certain age will remember the weather in the "old days" when London always seemed cool and damp the whole year. Now, we have climate change, and even the British weather isn't what it used to be.

In early June 2016, I was taking a break from writing this book when I checked the news on the Internet – "Heavy rain, the Seine rose 5.5m and Paris is flooded." Oops, I was going to Paris on holiday the following week! Then I remembered watching the news at the end of December 2015: masses of flood warnings in Northwest England. I also remembered doing a series of workshops in Dorset during February 2014 and wondering whether I would be able to get home because of the floods. The weather appears to be getting worse and more uncertain every year. Now, weather is serious business in Britain;[2] the uncertainty means not only do we have more to talk about, we are also having our lives disrupted. Let's face it, after you have been flooded out of your house three times in a decade because of a recurring "flood of the century," you'd start believing something uncertain (and unpleasant) is happening in the atmosphere.

Climate and environmental scientists tell us that global climate change is occurring because we are burning too much fossil fuel, and the resulting greenhouse gases are trapping the heat from the sun. (Detractors claimed otherwise; now there's uncertainty! Who do you believe?) The scientists claimed the result of climate change is more than just weird and unpleasant weather; it also contributes to crop failure and desertification of marginal land. With the prospect of polar ice cap melting, the impacts will include rising sea levels threatening low-lying islands and coastal regions; it also means that polar bears will be having a pretty hard time.

Now, there are all kinds of people who reckon this is a conspiracy by _____ (insert your favourite conspirators; the Internet will always be able to provide some degree of proof!), but actually whether it is climate change or the rain gods being unhappy with us, the reality is that people's lives are being damaged and their livelihoods threatened. By people, I mean people like you and me. It may not have happened to you (or me) yet, but hey, it can threaten our social fabric, and it can make the lives of our children and grandchildren more miserable too.[3] However, Greg Chant-Hall, an international expert on sustainability, suggests that people in different parts of society see sustainability as different things, and the different interpretations can contribute to uncertainty and lead to confused and mutually incomprehensible conversations. Groups are staking out different areas of society and confront each other with their own versions of the truth. Figure 1.3 uses the Triple Bottom Line sustainability model (described later in this chapter as well as in Chapter 3 and Appendix 2) to illustrate the divergence of views.

It is actually quite surprising that we have come this far with these very different views about what sustainability is. But joking aside, if we want our businesses to create wealth and jobs; if we want to see an end of human-generated species extinction; and if we want our society to be successful, then we need to take this seriously.

Countries and governments have been working on this for years, and in November 2015, 185 countries came together in Paris to agree to combat climate change, and the resulting Paris Agreement (also known as COP 21) brings the world's countries towards a common cause. The central aim of the Paris Agreement is to address the threat of climate change by keeping global

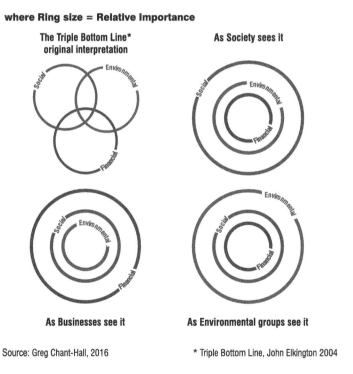

Figure 1.3 How Different Stakeholders Interpret Sustainability.

temperature rise to below 2°C from pre-industrial levels and furthermore, to pursue efforts to limit this rise to within 1.5°C.[4] The 1.5°C aim is to protect low-lying areas and island nations, which are more under threat from rising ocean levels. By May 2016, 177[5] countries signed the Paris Agreement, and by November 2016, it came into force. While this is good news to some, it is also anathema to others. President Trump announced that he will reduce the budget of the US Environmental Protection Agency, and people are now saying he doesn't believe in sustainability.

So what has this got to do with Everyday Sustainability? These are all high level things that we as individuals do not seem to be able to have much influence over. Unfortunately, an underlying cause for these concerns, the subsequent activities and legislation is Climate Change, and its impacts are all too real and can affect our lives and our businesses.

Climate Change, formerly known as global warming,[6] is a concern to the global community, as it not just impacts us next week when you are expecting a sunny holiday (like me) but also the way our organisations function. Thanks to globalisation, climate impacts can affect businesses around the world. I remember tracking the shipment of my newly purchased laptop only to find that it was stalled in the Far East because of a typhoon. In 2011, flooding in Thailand disrupted global supply of computer hard discs, and the 1995 and 2016 earthquakes in Japan disrupted just-in-time deliveries. We need to pay attention to climate change because it can affect our business activities, because our customers are concerned, because the media continually draw our attention and because our governments are putting in legislation to reduce the use of fossil fuels since citizens and media are concerned.

How did we get here?

To understand how Climate Change generated uncertainty and opportunities, we need to gain an understanding of the history of modern sustainability, also known variously as energy efficiency, environmental management, sustainability management or ecological management. The range of names gives us an indication of the possible opportunities for individuals and businesses to respond.

Modern concerns about Climate Change (or as it was called then, the Oil Crisis) started in 1973 when oil prices went from about US$0.80 a barrel to about US$3.00 a barrel. Uncertainty about the impacts of this (it was an abyss time, for sure) started a lot of actions that led to our current thinking on sustainability. That price rise set off major action in developed countries towards energy efficiency. The impetus in those early days was mainly on costs, rather than environmental protection. However, the focus has changed gradually. Figure 1.4 is my time line on the evolution of sustainability – it is not definitive or comprehensive, but it helps me understand how we got here.

A Sustainability Timeline*
from establishment to maturity

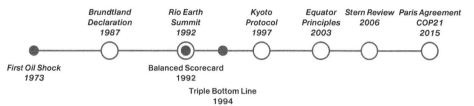

Figure 1.4 A Sustainability Timeline.

The Brundtland Declaration document for the United Nations in 1987 was called "Our Common Future." It is not a scintillating read, but it did establish the fact that we need to look after the world for future generations. This set the theme for sustainability as a real issue and framed its developmental pathways thereafter.

The Rio Earth Summit of 1992 established the principle that environmental protection should be a part of the development process.[7] It is a logical step from the thinking from the Brundtland Declaration and brought sustainability into real activities, rather than staying as lofty principles.

In the same year, Kaplan and Norton[8] introduced the Balanced Scorecard (see Appendix 2 for more details) as a management tool. I consider this a part of the evolution of sustainability, because this made it clear that business isn't just about managing profits, but also about managing customers, the staff and the processes. However, between management thinking and sustainable development, there was still a need for a lot of joining up.

Management thinking and sustainable development started to become linked in 1994 through John Elkington's Triple Bottom Line[9] model, where profits, people and planet are treated as equal elements in good management. This brought in social and environmental aspects together with economic/ financial aspects in a management framework. This model suggests that effective management means focussing on three areas equally: economic or financial areas, social areas and environmental areas. This then led to extensive debate on which of the three should be first.[10] Nonetheless, while Elkington's approach was still mainly seen as part of the evolving thinking on sustainability, the convergence with mainstream management thinking has started but was still not happening particularly quickly.

I remember following the news releases about the Kyoto Protocol in 1997 where it brought in legally binding national carbon dioxide (CO_2) targets.[11] This made sustainability official and part of government programmes and encouraged initiatives from green political parties and activists.

The Equator Principles of 2003 brought sustainability to project finance and capital finance. The Principles required capital projects to take into account the environmental impacts of their planned activities. As these were originally set up by a consortium of banks and other lenders, convergence was coming to the people who make the big investment decisions.

The 2006 Stern Review, all 600 plus pages of it,[12] made it clear that everyone is affected by climate change, and it does not matter whether you are rich or poor, or living in Europe or Asia, you'll get hammered in due course. Lord Stern, however, recommended solutions that included carbon pricing, deploying new technologies and energy efficiency. These shaped my thinking for Everyday Sustainability.

These activities led, in 2015, to the Paris Agreement or COP 21. Although, at the moment, I don't think a lot of people in the UK know whether our government has ratified the COP 21 Agreement (yes we have, on 18 November 2016) or whether it has drawn up any practical guidance or new legislation to demonstrate its strategy towards COP 21.[13] There is too much uncertainty in the world right now to worry about stuff like this.

Now, the thing about uncertainty, as mentioned earlier, is that we often treat these times as special and therefore react perhaps less rationally because "it is an emergency," "we need to get over this first" or "this *is* special." So, we get into panic reactions: spend wildly to get us out of the situation just when we should be a bit more careful with our budgets or going in the opposite direction with belt-tightening and recruitment freezes, just when we may need the talent and investment.

What's worse, sometimes the special times can lead to suspending a lot of the good working practices to deal with the "emergency," or stopping training and product development to help us preserve cash.

Unfortunately, in times of uncertainty, every day can bring unexpected changes (during the Easter weekend in 2017, how many of us in the UK thought there would be a General Election announcement immediately afterwards?). We cannot suspend good practice to accommodate "special times" when "special" readily becomes the everyday norm. Also, suspending good practice is not always a good idea, especially if it gives the impression that panic is setting in instead of "firm determination to see this through."

For example, global inflation seems to be gathering steam, with the oil producing nations again trying to cut production to force up energy prices. For many organisations, oil at say, $100/barrel, is a significantly bigger hit on the costs of doing business than $50/barrel.[14] So, how will your organisation manage if oil prices go up again? What preparations would you need to make to ensure your competitiveness is not hampered?

It is not enough to say that all your competitors will also be hammered by higher prices because such an attitude does not get your organisation "ready" for any challenges thrown up by uncertainty, nor does it boost your competitiveness? Unfortunately, cutting back is also not a good way forward since you are denying your organisation the opportunities you can exploit solution. Therefore this does not bode well for the sustainability of your organisation.

My suggestion for uncertain times is to not necessarily throw money and resources around, since few organisations have sufficient money to throw around, nor to get into a bunker mentality and sit out the storm. But instead I ask you to think about how your organisation works, to look at how it adds value and where it is creating waste. My experience with businesses, whether industry, service or public/third sector, led me to suggest that at least 10 per cent of costs can be recovered through a reduction of waste. Now, 10 per cent of cost can mean a great change to the profitability margin, even if you are Apple.[15] Through the lens of uncertainty, waste becomes even more critical: Waste mean we reduce our resources to deal with any changes brought about by uncertainty. Waste in money, time, effort and ideas reduce our effectiveness in dealing with uncertainty, and it certainly reduces our efficiency too.

It seems to me, therefore, the easiest, simplest and most practical way to get your organisation ready to take advantage of any opportunities thrown up by uncertainty is to reduce waste. Similarly, reducing waste will strengthen the structures of your organisation, all the better to deal with any threats from uncertainty. Finally, reducing waste actually recovers money currently lost to the organisation – what's not to like?

What are you saying? Not throwing waste paper away or printing out emails will save us 10 per cent of our costs?

Waste is more than paper; it is time (which costs money), it is effort (which costs money), it is materials (which costs money) and it is about the talent and ideas of your colleagues (which costs money). Waste is about the invisible delays, the re-doing of work, the unnecessary changes, the equipment sitting idle, the inconsistent outputs and things like make-work. Basically, waste is anything that the customer does not want or would not voluntarily pay for. Everyday Sustainability is about dealing with these kinds of waste. I will show you, through this book, how to eliminate waste.

The UK Government reckoned that there are six main ways of dealing with waste, and these were outlined in a Waste Hierarchy in 2000.[16] Figure 1.5 is a composite diagram that shows what I think the Waste Hierarchy means for the various stakeholders, and I suggest that there will be winners and losers among these groups.

The government's preference is clear – everything but landfills, because they are eyesores, they are filling up, they lose votes and they can cause ground water contamination. Incinerators are equally unloved because they can cause toxic pollution and especially since they also cost votes. Therefore, recycling looks the most likely solution (and it can be regulated by the government locally).

From an organisation's perspective, anything that doesn't cost money is preferred, but designing out waste is hard to do, and reducing waste means changing behaviour. So the option is to recycle. But let's have a closer look at the Waste Hierarchy.

If you **Design Waste Out** of your system: corporate structures, processes, procedures, building fabric, transport logistics etc., then life is good; you do

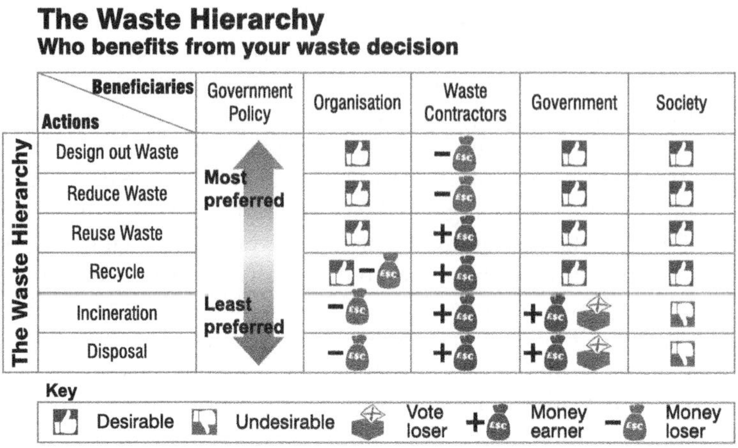

The Waste Hierarchy
Who benefits from your waste decision

The Waste Hierarchy — Actions \ Beneficiaries	Government Policy	Organisation	Waste Contractors	Government	Society
Design out Waste	Most preferred	Desirable	− Money loser	Desirable	Desirable
Reduce Waste	Most preferred	Desirable	− Money loser	Desirable	Desirable
Reuse Waste		Desirable	+ Money earner	Desirable	Desirable
Recycle		Desirable − Money loser	+ Money earner	Desirable	Desirable
Incineration	Least preferred	− Money loser	+ Money earner	+ Money earner, Vote loser	Undesirable
Disposal		− Money loser	+ Money earner	+ Money earner, Vote loser	Undesirable

Key: [Desirable] Desirable   [Undesirable] Undesirable   Vote loser   +£$C Money earner   −£$C Money loser

Figure 1.5 The Waste Hierarchy.

not waste resources and so save energy, protect the environment and "do" sustainability. And you also save money, which gives you more flexibility and options in your strategy.

Reducing waste is also good, but although you will try to use your resources as effectively as possible, some of them will end up as waste. Therefore, a bit more money has gone out of the organisation and a bit more effort has to be expended to reduce the waste.

Reuse is good too, but you would need to allocate space to store materials for reuse and assign corporate resources to manage it. This means a bit more effort and cost. There is also a limit to how much you can reuse without reprocessing.

Beyond Reuse, we need to remove the waste from the organisation, whether **Recycle**, **Incineration** or **Disposal** to landfills. Getting rid of your waste means interactions with all kinds of external bodies including: waste contractors, regulators and tax collectors, and one thing they all have in common is that they all have their hand out wanting some money from you.

Waste contractors

These people make money on your waste. It does not really matter whether it is waste for disposal or waste for recycling; they charge you for what they haul away. So any waste reduction or reusing of resources means their income is cut. It is not surprising that in the final analysis, waste reduction or elimination is not in their economic interest, no matter what they say.

Government

To me, the government's role in your waste decisions is contrary. On the one hand, the government is there to protect society from hazards, pollution, risks and so on. But on the other hand, it also makes money from taxation and fines. So they will want to restrict some of your activities, but they can lose tax income if you become too efficient. In some instances, governments can also lose votes if they are too lax in enforcing environmental legislation.

And what about society?

Efficiency and effectiveness are generally welcomed by society, but they are invisible. Trucks full of waste clogging the streets are visible, and landfills and incinerators send a shudder of dread over the community as well as depress the local real estate market. Therefore, although society generally appreciate good business designs (until their jobs are designed out) and waste reduction (and also until some pointless roles are removed), the invisible relief is often not noticed, and there is rarely any public joy in celebrating good practice.

Reuse in domestic situations appears different to reuse in business, and, as such, it may seem a more unfamiliar concept even though society does practice reuse at home – we all reuse containers, jars, bottles and plastic bags. At home, however, this is often somewhat ad hoc and tends to be less organised than it is at work. But overall, society sees reuse as a good thing.

Recycling, however, is a different matter. At home, we receive regular exhortations from local government and our trash haulers on the karma points we get from recycling, and they also make it "easier" by providing us with special bags and bins. Householders pay for domestic waste in fixed fee contracts (often as local services taxes), but larger organisations tend to pay for their larger waste loads by weight and are charged accordingly by the waste contractor and the tax authorities.

Going back to your organisation, however, the objectives are quite clear: Whatever your mission statement is about, giving more money than necessary to the waste contractor is unlikely to be an item on that list. Similarly, no organisation wants to pay more waste-related tax, like the Landfill Tax in the UK, than they have to.

Therefore, the focus for any organisation needs to be reducing whatever actions lead to waste and to optimise whatever activities add the most value.

We now start to look at Everyday Sustainability and the easy, simple and practical things you can do to make it happen.

Notes

1 Apologies for the mixed metaphors; it was hard to resist.
2 Weather is more than a mere conversation starter in the UK. *The Daily Mail* reckoned in 2010 that people in Britain spent 49 hours a year talking about the weather. (Source: Daily Mail website 14 May 2010.)
3 And science fiction movies have long depicted such grim futures. For example, in *Blade Runner* (1982), climate change resulted in endless rain, or in *Waterworld* (1995) the entire world was more or less underwater.
4 Source: United Nations Framework Convention on Climate Change. You can find the details of COP 21 if you search for it on the Internet. I do not provide

a link because the page changes regularly and any link I list will likely be a 404 error (page not found).

5 Early signatories included many small island countries (no surprises here) as well as Somalia and the State of Palestine.

6 It is not called that in Britain anymore because people liked the idea of warmer weather: "Hey! It's going to be like Italy, right?"

7 "Development process" is often a euphemism for government-level investment funding. It can be state sponsored or via inter-governmental agencies like the World Bank or sometimes philanthropy from very rich people and institutions.

8 These guys also brought us activity-based costing in 1988.

9 This is from John Elkington's Triple Bottom Line article originally published in the *California Business Review*, winter edition, 1994.

10 Should it be People, Profit and Planet; Planet, People and Profit; or any of the six possible combinations?

11 Although I never found out what happened if you missed the targets. Do you get sent home from the United Nations National Assembly? Or do you get fined? If so, who gets the money? (And what do they do with it?)

12 Disclosure: I've not read it cover to cover, as the 30-plus page Executive Summary was enough to overwhelm me – needless to say, it was not a scintillating read either. The proper name of this tome is "The Economics of Climate Change."

13 The answer to that one depends on what you consider practical. The UK Government's Energy Innovation Programme is available at www.gov.uk.

14 Oil prices in September 2014 and April 2017, respectively.

15 The *Financial Times* reported on 5 March 2017 that Apple has a margin of about 40 per cent.

16 UK Waste Strategy 2000. It is somewhere in the UK Government archives, but you can get hold of the Waste Hierarchy document through the www.gov.uk search engine.

2 Energy Productivity – how are you using energy at work?

We use energy in everything we do at work: We use energy to make things that we reckon our customers want – products and services that we then provide to our customers. Now, most of us carry out these activities within buildings,[1] and these buildings are fitted with various technologies that make our jobs creating these products and services easier: heating, ventilation, air conditioning, lighting, welfare facilities[2] and also amenities such as bike sheds. While the law states that welfare amenities are required in any workplace, it is also clear that these things do not actually add to the functional utility of the products and services. Having a place to rest and eat meals does not make an insurance policy any more comprehensive nor will it make the hi-fi equipment sound better. Similarly, having an effective payroll system does not make the refrigerators work better, although it is likely that the workforce may be happier.

This brings us to the understanding that there are two types of "useful" activities taking place at work: activities that deliver the goodies to the customers and activities that help make delivering the goodies easier and/or better. In jargon terms, these two activities are called value adding and value enabling, respectively. In theory, there is no reason why a customer should pay for value-enabling activities at your workplace, because they do not add to the usefulness or the functionality of the products or services. In practice, however, customers tend to be quite sanguine about paying for value-enabling activities, as long as the overall price does not appear outrageous (and your boss was not caught out publicly in a salary/expenses scandal). There is also a third type of activity that takes place at work – this is waste. Waste happens in virtually all organisations, and the penalties are lost time, effort, money, resources or productivity. Waste can also sap the workforce's morale. This concept of value and waste is shown in Figure 2.1.

Just as we can divide valuable work into two categories, we can divide energy use at work into the same two categories. I call these Operational Energy and Systems Energy, respectively. Operational Energy is used to create or make the products or services or value adding work. Systems Energy is used for value-enabling work.

Figure 2.2 shows the two types of energy as well as examples of the activities the energy is used for.

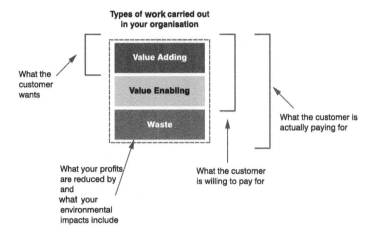

Figure 2.1 Redefining the Work Carried out Every Day.

Figure 2.2 Value-Adding/ Value-Enabling Work.

The definition of value-enabling activities can become ambiguous in some circumstances. Doesn't quality assurance (as it says on the can) ensure quality products? Don't adequate lighting and a pleasant working environment contribute to fewer errors and therefore higher customer satisfaction? Yes to both, but neither impacts the utility of the product or service. Having quality assurance in the assembly process would not make the motor of the fridge work better – it may reduce assembly errors, but if the basic design is awful, then an error-free assembly will not help much.

The link between energy use and waste is very simple: When energy is wasted, the money you paid for the energy is wasted; all the efforts (and energy used) in generating and getting those particular kWh to you are also wasted; furthermore, your environmental footprint is made bigger.

As I suggested in Chapter 1, the objective is very simple when dealing with waste – eliminate! Unfortunately, this is much easier said than done, because waste is not always obvious, like a leaking tap or lights left on in an unused room. Sometimes, you wouldn't know if waste is being created[3] in your everyday business processes. Toyota[4] reckons that anything that does not add value for the customer is waste. Now, that is a bit too black-and-white, since we proposed that value-enabling activities should not be considered waste. Nonetheless, since value-enabling activities are not necessarily adding direct value or utility to the customers, we need to optimise them.

To eliminate waste and optimise value-enabling activities, your processes need to be both efficient and effective. Being efficient is about using the right amount of resources or inputs to meet the customers' needs, and being effective is actually achieving that target. A simple way of assessing these two factors is by looking at a process' Overall Effectiveness,[5] or OE for short.

OE is made up of three component factors: the Availability of the resources to deliver or enable value, the Performance of these resources in the business processes and activities, and the Quality of the outputs.

Overall Effectiveness rate = Availability rate × Performance rate × Quality rate

These three factors encompass the operational spectrum of customer fulfilment, and OE is a very simple, but useful, way to analyse how well a process is running (Figure 2.3).

The relationship between OE and Efficiency/Effectiveness is shown in Table 2.1.

We can extend the exploration further by considering how we design and plan our processes. Conventionally, when people first think about a process, they focus on the Quality and assume 100 per cent Availability and Performance, whereas any realistic analysis will quickly show that a lower than planned Availability and Performance rate will quickly reduce OE.

Often, process and operations design and plan on a nearly 100 per cent Availability rate, a somewhat lower Performance rate (think about project slack and buffers) and perhaps accept a Quality rate in the low to mid-90 per cent range. However, while we take these into account in operations, we do not often extend these calculations into energy use. The impacts of an inefficient and ineffective process on energy use, shown through the OE elements, are described in Table 2.2.

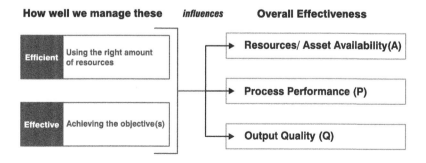

Figure 2.3 Effective and Efficient.

Table 2.1 Exploring Overall Effectiveness

	Efficient	*Effective*
Availability	Making sure the right amount of resources are available when they are needed	Making sure the resources are easily accessible and the assets are well maintained (or people have the right skills)
Performance	Designing out potential problems in the process	Making sure robust problem-resolution procedures are in place
Quality	Delegating quality management to the appropriate level (e.g. front-line teams)	Making sure the teams with responsibility are adequately trained and have sufficient resources to deal with quality variations

Table 2.2 Overall Effectiveness and Energy

	Operational Energy Impacts	*Systems Energy Impacts*
Low Availability	Fewer resources are available to work, so less energy is needed, but to achieve the target, overtime is probably needed	Resources are not available to optimise energy use overall Overtime means more Systems Energy is needed
Low Performance	Lower pace means less energy is used, but to achieve the target, overtime is probably needed	Resources are not available to optimise energy use overall Overtime means more Systems Energy is needed
Low Quality	Rework/rectification means more process cycles and more energy use	The need for rework/ rectification means energy is wasted

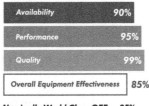

**World-Class Performance
Conventional Levels in Manufacturing**

Availability	90%
Performance	95%
Quality	99%
Overall Equipment Effectiveness	85%

**Nominally World Class OEE = 85%
(or A, P and Q all at 95%)**

Figure 2.4 World-Class Performance in Manufacturing.

While the impacts of low OE are fairly obvious, the energy impacts tend to be hidden, as people do not always link energy usage and waste to everyday activities.

For comparison purposes, an 85 per cent score in Overall Equipment Effectiveness in manufacturing is considered to be at "world class." The nominal numbers usually used as a yardstick are shown in Figure 2.4. How do you think your organisation measures up against this?

Overall Effectiveness and Energy Productivity

When I was working on the London 2012 Olympics programme, I was talking about OE to a team of electrical contractors fitting out an apartment block. I was told that because of various communications delays, the team of nearly 100 spent about 45 minutes or so waiting for instructions each morning before they started work. This is almost 75 hours waiting each and every morning! I subsequently used that conversation and other similar ones as examples of waste during my training workshops. Not surprisingly, examples like these resonated strongly with the various construction teams (Figure 2.5).

These waste situations come from work, whether at construction sites, shops, warehouses or offices. Such inefficient and ineffective processes are costing us not just money, effort and time, but literally also costing us the earth![6] Unfortunately, much of this is hidden from our immediate attention. When you are waiting for something to happen, or when you are rushing to get a job done, or when you are looking at a potential disaster (or having one pointed out to you), you are unlikely to ponder about OE or energy use – you are probably thinking more about how you can get out of this mess.

In Chapter 1, I introduced the Triple Bottom Line model of management. Figure 2.6 shows how this model applies to energy use and its associated costs.

Figure 2.5 Example of Hidden Waste.

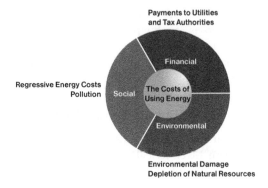

Figure 2.6 Energy and the Triple Bottom Line.

Energy, like all the resources we use, has a financial cost as well as a social and environmental cost. The financial costs are easy to notice, because we get bills from our utility suppliers. Environmental costs are more noticed these days because of society's growing awareness of the global impacts of industrialisation and resource exploitation. Whether we associate these with our activities probably depends on our own awareness of the underlying impacts of our work. Social costs are less visible, but they do exist: poor use of systems energy: poor lighting, wretched ventilation and so on can contribute to reduced productivity, whereas artificial cost subsidies in energy prices can affect the whole concept of efficiency. At a higher level, the application of fracking, for example, causes local, national and international tensions. A different problem with high energy costs is that it is regressive – the poor spend more of their income on energy than the rich. This can stifle innovation, and it can also cause social tension. Then there is pollution from fossil fuel use, which is often mentioned by the media in reports about bad air costing lives.[7]

So, how should we measure energy waste at work? Since energy is essentially invisible to us in everyday activities, one way to look at the hidden energy waste is to imagine energy as a derivative of the things we do. A systematic approach to examining energy use is to assess its productivity. This is shown in Figure 2.7.

Productivity is often described as the relationship between inputs and outputs, or something like

$$\text{Productivity} = \frac{\text{Outputs}}{\text{Inputs}}$$

We are familiar with the concept of labour productivity expressed as "outputs per employee" and also other productivity measures such as "numbers of cars produced per worker" or GDP per person. This concept is also used in measuring "profitability per employee" or "earnings per employee" or "earnings per share" as a measure of an organisation's prowess.

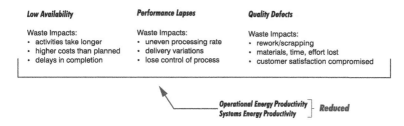

Figure 2.7 Examples of Hidden Waste and the Hidden Energy Footprint.

However, we are looking at how productive we are in using energy at work, so the approach needs to be based on outputs and energy used or

$$\text{Energy Productivity} = \frac{\text{Outputs}}{\text{Energy Used}} \text{ or} = \frac{\textit{Value Added}}{\text{total kWhs}}^{8}$$

Value Added is usually defined as the amount left over after material and overhead costs are subtracted from sales. It can also be expressed as the amount of money available for the company to spend as profits, wages, tax, depreciation, interest payments and so on.

(Note: We now have the confusion of Value Added and *Value Added*. I will use the italics version solely in describing Energy Productivity (EP) and the plain version for operations and process.)

The EP Key Performance Indicator (KPI), described above, is essentially how much money the organisation makes for every kWh (kilowatt-hour – a term describing unit power) used. This allows us to explore how an organisation is doing in terms of getting the most out of its energy use. Since energy use is partly an indication of how we are running our organisation, we use the EP KPI as an indicator of our Everyday Sustainability progress.

This allows us to assess our organisation on a regular basis without resorting to arcane assessments, complex derivatives or creative accounting procedures. Furthermore, because all the numbers are readily available for accounting purposes, it is even easy to do as well (Figure 2.8).

Changes in the *Value Added* figures can show both the impacts of waste and the benefits of being efficient and effective. One component that is likely to have the most impact is waste; we have already described that waste is the "*anti*-anything good," and basically everyone gets hammered by waste.

Waste from poor materials management, as well as inefficient use of overhead resources, will take a bigger chunk out of the sales income. It not only reduces profits, but it also makes it harder to get full value from the human and other resources. Waste makes indirect taxes even more costly, because even though you are not getting the full benefits from your resources, your tax rate does not drop accordingly. Similarly, interest payments become tougher as your cash flow and cash-in-hand are reduced by waste.

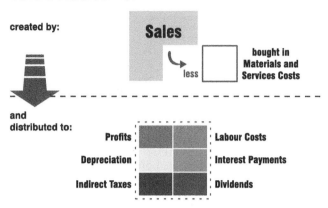

Figure 2.8 Value Added.

While asset depreciation happens whether you use the asset or not, waste is created when you do not get full value from the original purchase, despite being written off financially. So even if the impact of *Value Added* may be neutral in the books, in reality it is not a good thing.

What about excess inventory? If you buy more materials than you can use, then inventory levels will go up, distorting your *Value Added*. In terms of EP, a lower *Value Added* will lead to a lower EP value. Why? Because holding more inventory means you will need to store it properly (unless you don't mind leaving it to the elements or losing it to damage and theft), and that will take energy such as lighting, controlled temperatures and so on. So your energy use will also go up.

Excess inventory is something of an anathema in process efficiency circles. One of Toyota's pet peeves is when manufacturers over-produce to build inventory, as this is seen as covering up process problems. Consider the example used by Toyota to illustrate this: "when there is a lot of water (inventory) in the river then the rocks on the bottom (process problems) are not visible." Excess inventory also ties up your cash-in-hand and thence reduces corporate flexibility.

What the Energy Productivity KPI tells you

In the first instance, EP tells you how much value you are adding from each unit of energy used. Since energy use underpins every economic activity, using energy effectively and efficiently means we are actually running the business generally quite well. Figure 2.9 shows how good management practices impacts the EP KPI.

The various parameters that contribute to optimising EP can also be applied to technology deployment, people and their behaviour and process management. These three factors are the core of Everyday Sustainability.

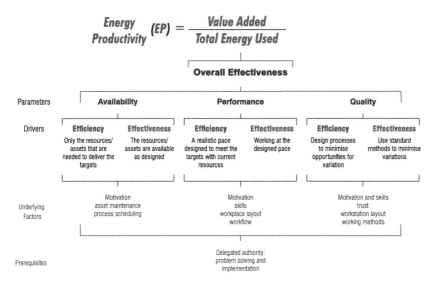

Figure 2.9 Integrated Framework for Optimising Energy Productivity.

When reviewed in this way, it is possible to see EP as an almost universal KPI, as the factors that result in a successful organisation are also the parameters that make up EP. Every department (or silo) in an organisation can be examined for its individual EP through the OE in its own specific areas. You would, however, require local metering to determine the energy used for each department's activities. This is described further in Chapter 3.

Assessing EP trends in your organisation can be carried out by selecting a base year or period (ideally one before the start of any improvement programme). This EP value then becomes the baseline, and you measure the changes by normalising all your figures to this baseline figure. The main benefits of doing it this way are twofold: you focus on the changes in EP performance, and your competitors cannot get a hold of your baseline value – they just weep when they see your EP trends ever upwards. See Figure 2.10 for an example.

Can we compare EP between different organisations in the same sector? In theory, it should be possible, as a larger organisation can be just as energy efficient as a smaller one. EP is a ratio, and the higher energy use of a larger organisation should be reflected in its larger value added. In reality, this may be more complex, as larger organisations may have more sophisticated or extensive energy technologies deployed, whereas a smaller organisation may be more cohesive in managing its daily use. Each of these brings benefits to EP values and also brings further factors to consider. Furthermore, larger organisations also carry a larger overhead in the energy use of its buildings.

Example

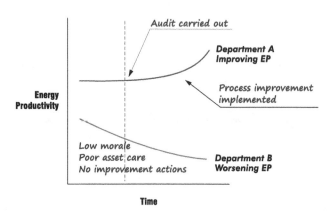

Figure 2.10 Energy Productivity KPI against Time.

Nonetheless, I believe that it is possible to compare EP performance between similar-sized organisations in similar sectors, and it will be useful in assessing loans or investment decisions. An organisation with a sound management (or improving EP) can mean a lower risk, and it may also mean that the loan or investment will provide a higher return.

A note on energy and carbon emission conversion factors

There are five main energy sources: coal, gas, oil, electricity and renewables. It is possible to explore and compare the impacts of our energy mix as well as to calculate the EP KPI. I have not included carbon emission numbers in this book, mainly to reduce the risk of confusion over fuel types and their usage. The UK Government publishes detailed tables on carbon-conversion factors at the following website (correct at the time of writing – April 2017):

> www.gov.uk/government/publications/greenhouse-gas-reporting-conversion-factors-2016

This provides kg CO_2 per KWh equivalent for the different fuels, and these can then be used to calculate a composite EP figure arising from the use of mixed fuels.

You may also find additional information from the UK Government at the Digest of UK Energy Statistics (DUKES) website (correct at the time of writing – April 2017):

> www.gov.uk/government/collections/digest-of-uk-energy-statistics-dukes

These emission-conversion factors are designed by the UK Government to "… to report on 2016 greenhouse gas emissions by UK based organisations of all sizes, and for international organisations reporting on UK operations…" (website url correct at the time of writing – April 2017):

www.gov.uk/government/publications/greenhouse-gas-reporting-conversion-factors-2016

Notes

1 There are exceptions; for example, construction workers and agriculture workers come to mind immediately.
2 The UK Health and Safety Executive states that employers need to provide the following welfare facilities: toilets and hand basins with soap and towels/hand-dryer, drinking water, a place to store clothing or changing facilities, if specialist clothing is needed for work; and somewhere to rest and eat meals.
3 There is a thought: We are actually spending time and effort making waste everyday – something that nobody wants.
4 You will find lots of references to Toyota Motor Corporation, because they invented Lean Thinking in the 1950s (which it called the Toyota Production System) and established the waste-reduction framework for everyone since.
5 OE is something I derived from Overall Equipment Effectiveness, part of Total Productive Maintenance, a maintenance approach from Denso Corporation (a part of the Toyota Group of companies). Also see Appendix 2 for more details.
6 Also the name of a 1991 book on sustainability by Frances Cairncross – well written and worth having a look to see how far managing sustainability has evolved.
7 For example, the *London Evening Standard* claimed on 28 April 2016 that 1000 Londoners were killed in four months by "London's toxic air;" and *The Economist* reported on 15 August 2015 that 1.6 million deaths/year in China were caused by air pollution.
8 Yes, major caveat here! It is not "energy," since it is kilowatt-hour and not joules, which is the proper unit for energy. But since you do not necessarily buy energy in megajoules, but instead in kWh, many people therefore treat kWh as energy used despite it being a derived unit of energy delivered at a constant rate over a period of time. For simplicity's sake, I will stick to using the term Energy Productivity (and kWh) and apologise to pedants everywhere.

3 Technology, people and process – the three components of Everyday Sustainability

Everyday Sustainability

The Stern Review suggested the way to make sustainability happen is via new technology, carbon pricing and energy efficiency. For those of us who are not rocket scientists, developing new technologies may not be feasible, but we can benefit by deploying the new technologies developed by other people. Carbon pricing and the intricacies of carbon trading may be beyond us (well, beyond me, certainly), but all of us can do energy efficiency readily (Figure 3.1).

Energy efficiency is, as its name says, about using energy efficiently or not wasting it. However, I suggest we extend this thinking a bit more to include using energy effectively too. It is fine to be efficient, but unless it is effective as well, all the efficiency in the world will not help you if you don't hit the target! Everyday Sustainability is about being both efficient (or using the right resources) and effective (or getting it right).

Everyday Sustainability is something real for us to aim for and achieve readily, because it is made up of three simple elements: using Technologies and our Capabilities in deploying them; managing People and their Behaviour; and Managing the Processes we use daily. While these three include plenty of management concepts, they are also much simpler than rocket science (Figure 3.2).

At first glance we seem to be on familiar ground: Technology has always been a big part of energy efficiency; behaviour, okay, touchy-feely stuff, has

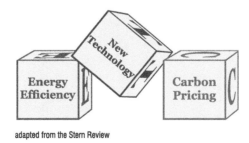

adapted from the Stern Review

Figure 3.1 The Three Building Blocks of Managing Climate Change.

Figure 3.2 Everyday Sustainability: The Three Connected Elements.

always had some role in saving energy; but wait, processes? What's that got to do with sustainability? Actually, quite a lot, and we'll get to them later in this chapter.

For this book, I don't want to talk about "technologies" or plant and equipment. This is because whatever technologies I suggest will be out of date by the time you read this book; so let's not waste time on a list of shiny but outdated kits that can help you. Instead, I suggest we look at how we can *use* the technologies, and to do that well, we also need to look at our capabilities. This brings us then to how we behave, respond and make decisions. You can buy the most efficient building management system in the world, but if people leave the windows and doors open, you are still likely to be wasting energy. The connections between technologies and people are therefore quite strong.

Processes – now there's a different matter. I worked with the UK government's energy efficiency programme in the 1990s and noted that managing processes was not mentioned in any meaningful way, if at all. Fair enough, not many people in the UK mentioned processes in the early 1990s. But I look at the publications from the energy saving sector and I still cannot find much mention of managing processes.[1] Why? This omission may contribute to wasting time, materials, energy, carbon, effort and cash at work.

Technologies and capabilities

What technologies are available? And how can they help you?

The answers for both questions can be either short and succinct or they can be never ending and full of technical jargon (i.e. boring to most people). I tend to opt for an easier life when I can, so let's go for the short and succinct.

Information on technology can be found in news media, popular technology media, sector-specific professional media, vendors/suppliers and also from professional bodies. Virtually any technology item can be searched for on the Internet, and you will get results. If you have nothing better to do, you can always ring a supplier, and you will then have new friends to talk to and all kinds of literature to read; you may even get visits from your new friends. There is nothing wrong with asking a supplier for advice, since they are likely to know more than you about the specific technology.

The hard part is knowing what you really need. For example, capital purchases of Information Technology systems and equipment have many examples of what happened when a customer was not too sure what they wanted and bought what they reckoned (or were told) would work.[2] This can, and has, ended in tears.[3] The technology options for energy efficiency may not have such drastic outcomes, but it can be just as difficult.

I suggest we look at technology simply as something that we, and our colleagues, are meant to use easily and perhaps (ideally) understand how it works too. This modest aim means that the capabilities of our people may be as important as our choice of technology.

It is always possible to train our people so that they can become fully proficient with whatever technology we are bringing in. However, a reality check (or just check the corporate budget) will suggest that maybe it is best to stick to technology our people can use or introduce technology and training in an incremental way that remains affordable.

Easy, simple and practical

Although having technology matching the capability of the workforce is good for the short to medium term; for the longer term, some aspirational element is also necessary. We do need to introduce changes, since technology does not stand still. However, I would suggest you plan your technology upgrade and its accompanying training with three broad aims:

Make it:

1   Easy to understand and learn

    Easy to learn is a "must" so people will not spend too long learning it. Ideally, they need to be able to pick up the salient points without misinterpretation or incomprehension. Reducing the time to learn also reduces costs too.

2   Simple to use

    This is critical because people will make mistakes if it is not simple to use. Not only is it embarrassing when people get the new technology wrong, it is also a poor return on investment.

If you are investing in new technology that is hard to learn and difficult to use, then you better make sure this technology makes a lot of sense to the people at work so that they are willing to spend time learning how to use it. Otherwise, the technology will be ignored, and people will resort to old technology through workarounds. This brings us to the final aim:

3   Making it practical

You need to make sure the technology is relevant to everyone, or, in other words, you need to get people to be bothered about using it and learn how to use it. In fact, if the new technology is not deemed relevant to the employees, they are likely to ignore it anyway – or only pay attention as long as you are watching them.

People and their behaviour – why can't people be bothered?

Often when people analyse a situation, they perceive, rightly or wrongly, that the efforts in doing whatever is being asked is more than any benefit or value *they* may receive. The two key words here are "perceive" and "they," and both hinge on the information they have to make the bothered/not-bothered decision.

A simple decision-making process is shown in Figure 3.3, but the outcome is always difficult to predict, as the value received differs for different individuals. There is the initial gut response – is this worthwhile to pursue? If the situation is unpalatable, it will not go beyond this step. Once it is decided that this situation may bring some benefits, then further exploration takes place.

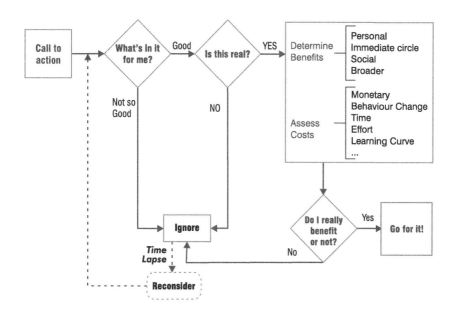

Figure 3.3 Breaking Down the Individual's Decision-Making Process.

This usually means gathering more information, and then some form of cost/benefit analysis takes place. This can become intense, with discussions and calculations; or more casual, with a quick mental assessment. Either way, it can be logical or emotional, tangible or intangible or a mix of all four.

We can segment these reactions into perceived outcomes that are either tangible or intangible, as well as logic- or emotion-driven decisions. The responses depend on what we think the outcomes will be, as well as how we arrive at our decisions. While the two matrices in Figure 3.4 offer a generic set of responses under each set of conditions, the difficulty is to predict whether an individual will be driven by logic or by emotions under any particular circumstance. Since we are all different, what is logical to me may be emotional to you, and although the tangible/intangible choice seems much easier in contrast, it still isn't necessarily the case, since we all look at things differently.

Since we cannot predict how other people will react or respond, we need to focus on what we can do to encourage a positive response to our proposal. Ideally, you want to present the information that helps people make a decision in your favour. This means several things: getting the message contents right for the intended audience, making sure there are no factual errors and delivering the message without ambiguity.

Luckily, Everyday Sustainability is about achieving outcomes that benefit not just the investors and the employees, but also the broader stakeholder community too. Figure 3.5 segments the stakeholder groups into three broad categories.

The Everyday Sustainability outcomes package of reducing costs, respecting the stakeholders and minimising environmental impacts brings plenty of rewards. Cost savings will preserve jobs, increase profitability and also mean more taxes for the government. Stakeholders can benefit from better working practices, workplace partnerships and more innovations, as well as the prospect of fewer accidents. Reducing waste means a lower carbon footprint and also less impact on global resources generally. In such a package, everyone should be able to find something that they can buy into.

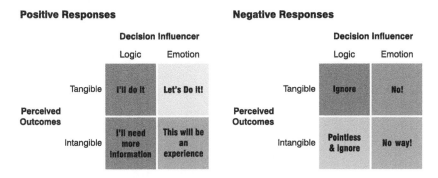

Figure 3.4 Positive and Negative Responses.

Note: a stakeholder can straddle more than 1 segment depending on specific point of interaction with you at any one time

Figure 3.5 Stakeholder Segments.

However, there will be instances where people just do not respond, and it may be because they cannot understand their role, or maybe it is because they are just feeling fed up. The responses can be split into an emotion-driven response or a logic-driven response. Figure 3.6 offers some familiar scenarios and their associated thinking and reasoning. The emotional responses may change after you make concerted efforts to raise their confidence in your initiative, as well as supporting and listening to their concerns. The logic-driven responses, however, may indicate something is not right structurally about mutual respect and trust in the organisation. And of course, these do not necessarily tie up with the headline response – especially the one who is saying yes just to get rid of you!

Having said all that, how the message is delivered can also influence the response and outcomes. We are familiar with this from our own experience, but let's just summarise the range of outcomes when something new or different is introduced. We know from childhood that the "it's for your own good" statement does not always result in short-term gains. We also know that we can deal and trade favours to get things done. Reasoning helps to an extent, but sometimes you get compliance only because you have worn them down. Now, since we have been responding to these "good for you" admonishments from childhood, we do know a thing or two about whether these approaches and styles would work or not work as well as those ones we like or dislike.

Our own personality, situation, experiences and mood therefore drive the style we choose to encourage participation – whether in a directive and bossy way, or via a more collaborative style or even the bureaucrat's

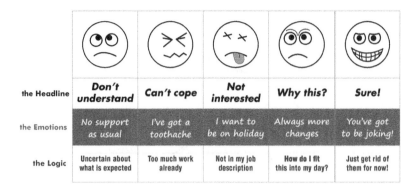

the Headline	*Don't understand*	*Can't cope*	*Not interested*	*Why this?*	*Sure!*
the Emotions	*No support as usual*	*I've got a toothache*	*I want to be on holiday*	*Always more changes*	*You've got to be joking!*
the Logic	Uncertain about what is expected	Too much work already	Not in my job description	How do I fit this into my day?	Just get rid of them for now!

Figure 3.6 Negative Outcomes – More than One Reason behind the Headlines.

favourite: seeking compliance through endless (and often incomprehensible) explanations, often in text and small print, of course. Similarly, they also drive our responses: supportive, negative, cynical and so on.

Managing processes – examining the way we work

Do our business processes inhibit good practice? Do the procedures result in more energy use (and waste)? Does the workplace layout contribute to errors and mistakes?

These are fundamental issues that can hamper our Energy Productivity even before we start work. These can be categorised into four main areas: hazards, discomfort, mismatches and dysfunctions (Figure 3.7).

Hazards are where our actions create risks and hazards for ourselves. Safety lapses and weak policies are fairly obvious hazards, but so is poor maintenance where equipment and plant can fail suddenly or catastrophically. These disrupt plans and operations by reducing the available assets (including people) to do the work and slowing down the pace of work, reducing our Overall Effectiveness and *Value Added.*

Discomfort is something that affects people directly: poor lighting, heating, ventilation, noise and dust particles all distract us from doing our jobs. These factors can result in us working slower and perhaps contributing to errors and mistakes. In more extreme cases, these can cause both short-term accidents and long-term illnesses from dust, noise, poor lighting and so on. These factors can also have an impact on equipment, as sustained high temperatures can lead to failures in electronic circuits,[4] or the breakdown of lubricants in moving machinery and so on, resulting in equipment failure.

Mismatch is about mismatch in human factors or ergonomics and also about a communications gap between different people that leads to such mismatches. Often, it is a mismatch between technology and its users – a

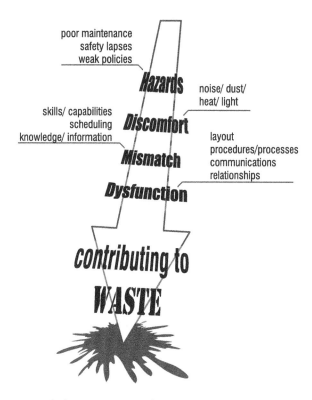

Figure 3.7 How Workplace Issues Contribute to Waste.

wrong match of technology against skills and capabilities; scheduling and planning systems that do not pay sufficient attention to people's needs and behaviour; and mismatch between knowledge and where it can be found and deployed.[5]

Dysfunction ranges from the workplace itself to people in the workplace. A poor workstation layout can lead to poor process flow, excessive movements and wasted movements. Dysfunctional workplace layout can mean energy spent in heating and lighting unused corridors, store rooms with lights permanently left on and so on. Processes and procedures that are not optimised waste resources, time and money, with people doing more and achieving less. Dysfunctional communications leads to errors and misinterpretations and can result in damaged relationships between different groups of people and thence splintering any effort towards improving energy productivity. Ask yourself, is your workplace's setup resulting in wasted energy?

We need to remember that a well-designed and functional working environment is essentially invisible – we do not notice it because such an environment makes our jobs easier to complete, and we move onto other tasks smoothly without the hassles that slow us down, introduce workarounds, contribute to errors and mistakes as well as make ourselves physically unwell.

Such a workplace can be achieved by gradually improving Energy Productivity through the various areas described in Figure 2.9. But like anything at work, if you leave it alone for any length of time, some problems will start to reappear, and, therefore, I would suggest a regular check on whether your workplace is sliding back towards poor performance.

Technology, people and processes

Can you do without any one of the three?

Technology costs money and we often don't have a lot of money available. This is a very good question, as organisations have to prioritise budget allocations. The energy efficiency campaigns of the last century always told us that money spent on energy-saving equipment was money well spent because a payback would come (very) soon from energy costs savings and the purchase would be the gift that keeps on giving year after year.[6] This theme had one problem: the people saying it were engineers like me but without much awareness of either opportunity costs or the cost of capital. Both these can shape how you invest and what you invest in. However, energy costs were very high in the 1990s, and perhaps a new bit of kit would help save money, but so would investment in training, sales or process plant.

Most organisations have some idea of their cost of capital and therefore some idea of how much income a project needs to generate to become an attractive option.[7] In the current climate of low interest rates, low inflation and low energy prices,[8] the numbers will still need to be crunched, but the lower cost of energy can mean energy savings from more efficient technology may no longer be the main reason for investment.

A simpler approach may be that where capital is expensive, invest in people, where labour is expensive, invest in technology. However, I am concerned that while energy-efficient technology is important, and stated by *The Stern Review* as one of the three pillars towards sustainability, I think it also dilutes the need for everyone to take responsibility for sustainability. To me, having a box humming in the corner with lots of dials and cables is similar to contracting-out your services – not your problem anymore. There is nothing wrong with this; energy saving is energy saving, but it just doesn't engage the employee, and without engaging the employee, we will not have Everyday Sustainability.

The old saying "Give a man a fish, and you feed him for a day. Teach a man to fish, and you feed him for a lifetime" is close to how I look at Everyday Sustainability. My proposal is that we should try, without major investment initially, just to get people to realise that sustainability is something we can all own and take part in. If your colleagues manage to reduce energy waste and save money, well, you can spend more towards the investment in energy technology equipment to save even more money (and energy).

You may get away with doing without high-tech investment in the short term, but it is not a long-term approach, as your competitors who invested will eat your lunch eventually. Nonetheless, low-tech improvements (i.e. cheap equipment and not major capital items) can contribute to enhancing our energy productivity, and often, they are more visible to the teams too.

What about people then? Can we drop this one and still optimise our Energy Productivity? What if we tell people that unless they comply with energy waste reduction, they'll be replaced by robots (or overseas outsourcing)? Will that work? We don't have to spend time (and money) doing all the touchy-feely stuff. This then makes energy waste reduction a conformance issue, like taxes or laws.

Most of us are law-abiding much of the time, but a lot of us also spend a lot of time and effort trying to minimise our taxation or help ourselves to items in the stationery cupboard. Some of us will try to game the organisation's system, believing that human ingenuity will always triumph over bureaucratic rules. You do not want sustainability to get to that level, because it is something that will affect not just us but also our families in the future, our friends and friends that we've not met yet. Reducing waste should not be something bound into a staff handbook. It should be something we do because it is the right thing to do. To make that happen, we need to engage people, help them overcome their fears and uncertainties and work in partnership to reduce waste.

So doing without people in sustainability is not on either. What about processes? Since most energy-efficiency programmes have not involved significant levels of process improvements, then clearly it is possible to ignore it. However, not bothering with processes will mean that real sustainable gains are not going to be achieved. Furthermore, since the reason for writing this book is to highlight the benefits of including process as a major element of achieving energy efficiency, I certainly will not encourage ignoring our processes.

To manage our processes, however, we will need technology to help us communicate effectively and to help us keep the workplace running smoothly. Energy technology can help us, because it provides us with the information to shape our decisions, it helps us manage our processes, and it can create a work environment that makes work easier. Optimised processes allow us not only to save energy but also to get the most from both our people and technology assets, while process management allow us to introduce improvements and innovations through engaging people and deploying equipment and technologies.

And people? People leverage technologies to get the most out of processes – energy-efficient motors, low-energy computer servers and better heating, lighting and air processing to give us a suitable environment to deliver value. So we will need people to take part, since they run the processes (or program the computers that run the processes).

In other words, to manage processes effectively and efficiently, you will need to integrate these with the management of people and technology. And to do that, we need to understand what is happening at work.

Notes

1 Sorry, no names mentioned, but you know who you are.
2 This also applied to domestic equipment, such as modern TVs, and remember the fun we had in (trying to) operate video recorders?
3 *The Guardian* reckoned on 18 September 2013 that the UK's national patient health record system had cost at least £10B for what would have been the world's largest civilian IT system, and it was ... er... abandoned when it didn't work.
4 Sustained heat can lead to diffusion of metal across solder joints, leading to voids and ultimately joint failure – trust me, I trained as a metallurgist!
5 A manager at a major UK company told me: "... I am sure we have pockets of excellence, but we just don't know where they are in our company..."
6 Trust me, we did say things like this in the 1990s.
7 Using metrics such as Return on Investment (ROI) or Internal Rate of Return (IRR).
8 If this is no longer true when you read this book, well, it's because of uncertainty!

4 Understanding what is happening at work

Before we can embark on our Everyday Sustainability programme, we need to have sufficient information to analyse and allow us to make effective solutions, so we really need to know what is going on at work.

Things we do every day

What are we doing at work besides putting out fires, pointless activities, waiting, sorting out changes to schedules and fixing someone else's mistakes? Ah, there is the day job, what we are hired to do. Whatever we are doing, we often work to some sort of procedure, and when the procedure falls over, we do a workaround (there is even a procedure in putting out office fires: don't panic, pass the buck and blame someone else). However, the reality of what we are doing at work does not always resemble what we think we are doing:

> A doctor at a London hospital decided to analyse the official 23-step process for a patient to see him for the first time. He "walked" the process and found that there were actually 154 individual steps between a patient's initial referral to finally seeing the doctor.

> A manager at a London housing association mapped the main business process and stuck it on the wall. Her team was astonished: "Is this how we actually work?"

If we are not sure how we actually do our work, how can we set realistic targets? And, even more importantly, how can we improve a process that is not necessarily real? This becomes critical when we are looking at achieving the targets or adding value. How can we tell we are actually doing something useful, since the foundations we are using as a baseline are suspect?

Furthermore, how do you decide what to do? Do we react and respond to events? Firefighting is a fact of life – sometimes we need to make an appointment with ourselves just to get some time away from dealing with all the other things that are going on! There is no shame in admitting what is a reality for quite a few of us. Of course, some of us are well organised, and we settle down to do the jobs we intended to do that day. But either way, how do we actually decide what to do? Do we

use our experience to help us make our decisions? Or
use our gut instinct to form the decision? Or
gather some information first and then work out the way forward?

We probably use all three, at different times, for different jobs. But when we are looking at how to improve the way we work, we need to look at this in a more logical way, as suggested in Figure 4.1. Both instinct and experience help us form the decision: whether it is sensible to continue, whether we can get it to work and so on. However, both instinct and experience rely on using information to frame the issues that need a decision. The contents of the information and the way it is used will shape the decision, as well as the outcomes.

Making decisions based on data and information is a fundamental aspect of Six Sigma Quality[1] management. Similarly, quantitative data (or numbers) can help us define a situation with less ambiguity and is applied in many process improvement approaches such as Lean Operations.[1] For example, how do the two situations in Table 4.1 compare?

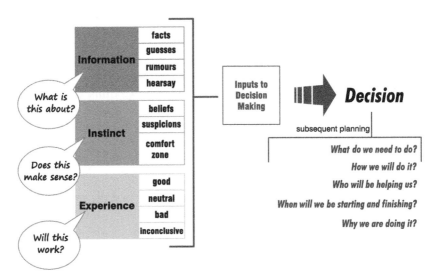

Figure 4.1 Analysing the Decision-Making Process.

Table 4.1 Answering Query

1 We answer customer enquiries quickly...	2 We answer customer enquiries quickly, with a response within the first 24 hours...

Table 4.2 Detailed Answers

1 We aim to answer customer enquiries quickly to provide a better service. We will implement this in the summer...	2 We aim to answer customer enquiries quickly, with a response within the first 24 hours for 95 per cent of our callers. We intend to deliver this level of service within three months from today, 15 June...

Both aim for a "quick" response, but what you may consider "quick" may not necessarily correspond to what your customers consider "quick." By providing the additional information, it becomes easier to judge the two service targets.

In the case of improvements, quantifiable information, such as "5 per cent improvement in quality," for example, helps us make decisions that are based on common data, rather than sorting through various different interpretations of "better."

But doesn't this turn us into robots with no emotions? Are we sprouting numbers just to satisfy our finance colleagues? Isn't this very un-cool? Well, maybe, but with budgets shrinking in most places, we need justification for our proposals. It is so much easier to decide how to go forward when there is sufficient information to help us make a more informed decision, as shown in the two continuing examples provided in Table 4.2.

Which of the two proposals provided in Table 4.2 is likely to be more useful in meaningful discussions and planning?

But in getting to the stage of providing the additional details shown above, information, instinct and experience are all part of the overall equation:

- **Information** allows us to describe what we plan to do, when we can deliver this and what outcomes are expected.
- **Instinct** tells us that three months is a likely time period for our colleagues to get their act together, and there should be less resistance to change compared to a big bang.
- **Experience** tells us that it will take some time to implement, as we are unlikely to get it working immediately, nor are we going to deliver a full 100 per cent service quickly.

By combining these three elements, we can prepare initial plans that contain useful details to our teams, as shown in Figure 4.1.

Value Adding and Value Enabling

A Value Stream Map,[2] or VSM, highlights the purpose of our work, as it shows the main blocks of value adding in a business process. It is a high-level process map that identifies the major activities to create or deliver value.

From a customer- or end-user angle, value is what use we get from the products or services that we acquire.

Often, when people think about processes, they tend to think in terms of activities that lead to outcomes or adding value, even when they are unaware of the jargon! They are visualising a VSM such as the example shown in Figure 4.2.

Nevertheless, many activities are needed to enable the delivery of value. In the case of the omelette example, these can include having enough eggs as well as having some idea about how to make an omelette. In our daily work, these activities can be something as simple as using a photocopier to let us copy documents, a room to sit down and have lunch in or even an effective payroll system to make sure that our pay arrives on time. These value-enabling activities generally do not improve the utility of the products and services, but they are necessary to ensure the smooth running of the organisation.

Earlier, in Chapter 2, we explored the concept of Operational and Systems Energy, and these are somewhat analogous to the value-adding activities and the value-enabling activities, respectively.

While the VSM is useful in telling us what we are doing, it does not go into detail of how we are doing it. This is where the Process Map comes in. A Process Map is a detailed step-by-step description of what is happening when we do our job. In our examples earlier of the doctor and the manager, it was the Process Map that led to the rather startling acknowledgement that they were not really doing what they thought they were doing.

Do note that the VSM does not include a lot of details that are revealed upon deeper exploration, as shown in Figure 4.3. Without these details,

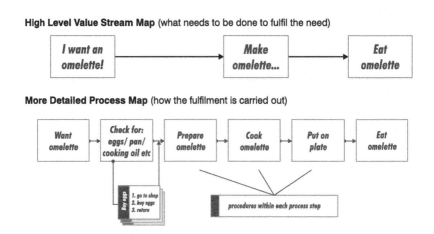

Figure 4.2 Value Stream and Process Maps Example.

some of the more optimistic targets suggested from a cursory look at the VSM (often by people not directly involved in the delivery) may not be achievable when all the unseen workarounds and bureaucratic functions are taken into account. And this is before we factor in the value-enabling activities.

Energy inefficiency is often a part of the inherent complexity of these hidden[3] activities, which offer potential for waste both in Operational and Systems Energy use. Process simplification is one way to ease this situation, but before we can simplify the process, we need to know what it is currently (the Current State), and that requires a detailed mapping.

Process Mapping is often created by walking[4] each step of the process, as well as logging what happens during each step. In this instance, it is not just logging physical assets but also operational details. The relationship between the VSM and the Process Map is shown in Figure 4.3.

Furthermore, Process Maps can also be used to describe other information such as the overall time taken in a very visual way through a scaled representation of the length of time for each step and also the time between two steps. Whilst this type of depiction is very useful in showing the overall lead time for any process, it is even more useful in showing non-value-adding time. Sometimes, the gaps between process steps are due to scheduling reasons, but often they can be just delays because of people carrying out their work in batches[5] (Figure 4.4). (There are also other obvious reasons for the long gaps between activities, but I don't have the time to tell you, because I'm on a coffee break now!)

The information you can gather on a Process Map goes beyond what people are doing during each step (and between the steps) to what is happening during that particular process step (Figure 4.5). The Six Sigma

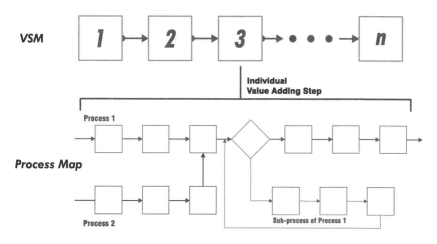

Figure 4.3 Value Stream Map and Process Map.

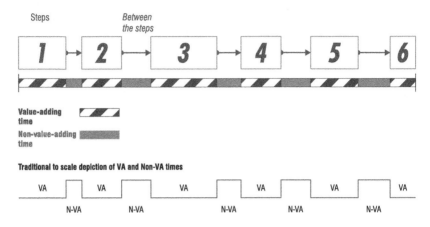

Figure 4.4 Process Steps Described in Terms of Time Taken.

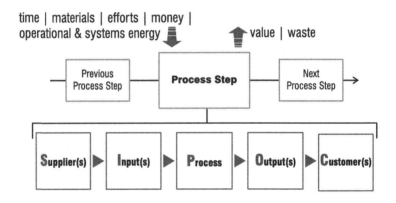

Figure 4.5 SIPOC – Analysing a Single Process Step.

tool SIPOC[6] is useful for analysing each step as it breaks the information into coherent and integrated segments that allow you to ask relevant questions, including:

Supplier – Who are they? What is their relationship to you? How often do they supply you? How do they actually deliver to you?...

Inputs – What are they? Are they what you needed? Are the amounts correct? Are they in a form you can readily use? How are they stored?...

Process – What do you do with the inputs? Is this what you expected to happen? Do the activities happen as planned? Are all the required resources there? Do you have the right skills for the job?...

Outputs – What are the outputs? Are they to specifications? What shape/state are they in? How are they stored/packaged/delivered?...

Customer – Who are they? Are they in-house or outside customers? Can they find the outputs? What will they do with the outputs? Can they contact you easily about your outputs?...

This analysis also allows us to look for problems and errors and the potential energy waste implications associated with every point of the process step. For example, storage options will contribute to Systems Energy use, and transport requirements will also impact both Operational and Systems Energy. SIPOC can contribute to focussing on aspects of storage and transport of both incoming and outgoing logistics, areas traditionally treated as outside the scope of the "process step." Nonetheless, these two areas can impact both energy usage and wastage.

In addition to the parameters listed above, you can also explore other factors such as skills and their development: the journey from knowledge, competence, capability to experience of the people involved. Figure 4.6 shows a simple explanation of these four elements.

These four factors are likely to contribute to determining how well the job is carried out and whether you can keep it up over time. Despite being well trained, a capable and motivated workforce can only work so many wonders with obsolete equipment. Similarly, people can put up with some tough situations in the short term for a valuable goal, but if this is dragged out, then motivation can slip, and with it, capabilities. After all, if an organisation is in

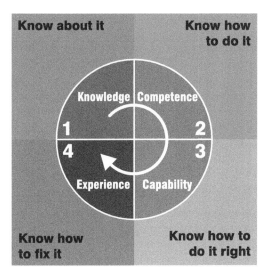

Figure 4.6 From Knowledge to Competence – A Journey of Development.

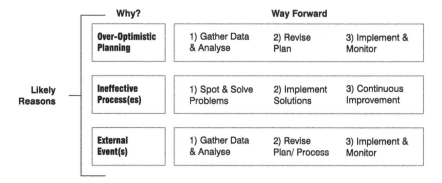

Figure 4.7 When Overall Effectiveness Is Lower than Expected.

perpetual firefighting mode, then there will be some doubts about the ability of the management, and it will be difficult for the staff to keep up their morale and their confidence in the management.

By deploying Process Mapping and SIPOC, you can gather a large amount of information about a particular process. An easy way is by starting from a set of headline Overall Effectiveness[7] metrics comprising

Asset Availability – Is everything there to allow the work to go ahead as planned?
Process Performance – Is everything working as designed?
Output Quality – Is the output at the required specification?

It is possible to gain a snap shot of how the Value Stream is running from this information. If the figures are in the expected range, then the emphasis should be on reducing costs, reducing errors and so on as part of continuous improvement. However, if the Overall Effectiveness is lower than expected (and it often is), then it is time to start examining why. Selecting and gathering data effectively are critical parts of Everyday Sustainability, and these topics are discussed in detail in Chapter 5 (Figure 4.7).

The current state

Workarounds are often temporary fixes to a small problem, and although people do not often see these as part of the proper process, they can become the *de facto* process. The problem is that if the workaround actually works (to a fashion), then busy people are often content to leave it alone and get on with their other tasks. This means that a temporary fix becomes a daily fixture and then evolves into "the way we do it here." If the team subsequently moves or rearranges the workplace, it is likely that someone will spot the unusual work arrangement brought by the workaround, but if the team is very busy, then things may carry on as before, and the process can become increasingly unwieldy.[8] In my experience, this is often the case for workarounds in most busy organisations. As for those places with a lot of time on their hands, well, a ponderous process may appear serendipitous instead, so what's the rush to fix it?

Therefore, yes, workarounds need to be included in the initial Process Mapping since that is how we work daily. The types of information gathered for a workaround should be the same as those for any "normal" process step, because that way, you have consistency in gathering your information. The energy used in a workaround may rise above that used in a normal process to reflect the additional activities.

Even if you are busy and running hard to catch up, you still need to identify the various bottlenecks and choke points in your process. A full Process Mapping is necessary to identify potential and actual issues, nevertheless a high-level VSM can also be used to spot likely problem areas. In these situations, you will need to map your Value Stream in terms of both activities and teams. An easy way to portray this is by using Swim Lanes, where the activities are segmented by various individuals or teams and their respective actions, as shown in Figure 4.8.

By representing your process in these Swim Lanes, it is possible to look for potential and actual choke points. Even before you walk a process, the Swim Lanes will give an indication of where you should focus. So, if all roads lead

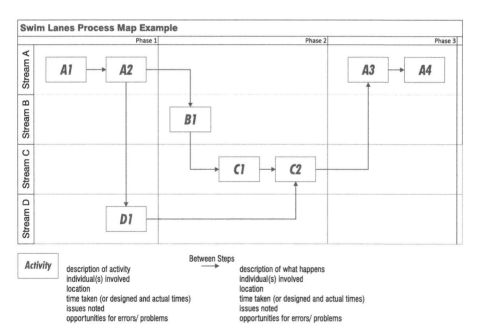

Figure 4.8 Swim Lanes Process Map Example.

to Rome, then a traffic snarl-up in Rome is likely to mess up all the traffic on all the other roads. Swim Lanes are also useful in exploring whether the snarl-ups will impact both Operational and Systems Energy use.

The Swim Lanes diagram in Figure 4.9 shows the relationship between different streams of activities. These can be from internal teams in both operational and support functions, as well as from external suppliers and contractors. In Lean Operations, there is an emphasis on "go and see" or "go to where it is happening,"[9] and since time is limited, this offers a quick start on where to go and spot problems.

When you design using Swim Lanes, the newly designed map also allows you to check whether the basic process design is likely to be robust, what type of communications framework is needed, how the relationship between the different streams of activities should be managed and whether the particular teams involved can deliver to the planned schedule (Table 4.3 and Figure 4.10).

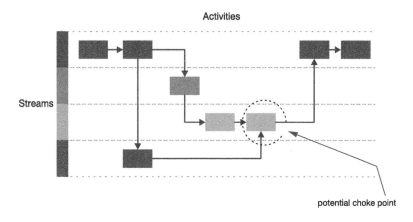

Figure 4.9 Swim Lanes and Potential Choke Points.

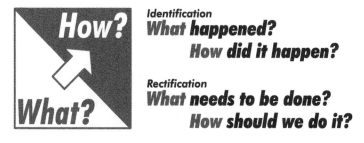

Figure 4.10 The What/How Matrix.

The What and the How

Once you have highlighted areas in the process that may become (or are) trouble spots, then the questions you should ask are provided in Table 4.3.

The What-How relationship is probably the foundation for improving Everyday Sustainability at work, as it provides a simple but structured framework to look at how technology, people and process can be integrated into useful and lasting solutions.

These two questions follow and drive each other, and the approach is applicable for problem identification, solution development and also initiating strategy and policy development. For example,

Problem identification at the working level:
> **What** is the reason for the process running slower than planned?
> And
> **How** shall we resolve this issue?

Solution development at the working level:
> **What** do we need to do to reduce the level of errors and mistakes in this process?
> And
> **How** shall we do that?

Strategy and policy development:
> **What** can we do to improve our Energy Productivity?
> And
> **How** shall we achieve this?

Each of these questions leads to a range of answers, and in many ways, this becomes a series of branches that increase in detail as we go further into the What/How analysis. A cascading Tree Diagram,[10] like the example in Figure 4.11, shows how details can be greatly increased by going further into the What/How analysis.

With the "What" identifying the likely action(s) needed and the "How" providing ideas on the activities to deliver these objectives, it is then time to explore how risky these activities are likely to be. Risk is relative, and everyone (and every organisation) has somewhat different levels of risk tolerance. Nonetheless, we need to be able to measure the impact of risks in a systematic way prior to making a decision on whether the risks are acceptable.

Table 4.3 Identification and Rectification

Identification	*Rectification*
What happened here?	What needs to be done?
And	And
How did that happen?	How should we do it?

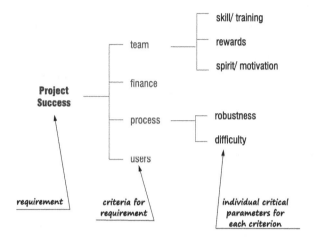

Figure 4.11 A Cascading Tree Diagram Example.

In Lean and Six Sigma, a common way to measure risks is the Failure Modes and Effect Analysis[11] or FMEA. This is a detailed risk-analysis methodology that integrates various aspects of risk management into a series of metrics, as shown in Figure 4.12.

The impact analysis from the FMEA can readily accommodate factors beyond operational parameters. The impacts can be examined using a Balanced Scorecard-style framework, and from there, the analysis of Everyday Sustainability elements can lead to further sets of questions.

After this series of analysis, you should have a fairly clear idea about What/How your processes are doing, as well as some indication to whether they are performing to design, to your expectations or to your customers' expectations. All of these are then able to support a process improvement from the Current State to the Future State. With all the information on the process gathered, it is time to check whether the technology and people factors need to be changed as well.

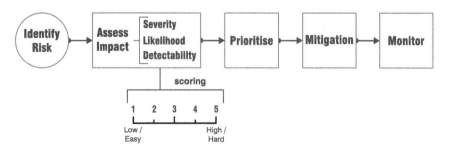

Figure 4.12 Failure Modes and Effects Analysis (FMEA).

Technology – the questions to ask

Generally, just about every energy supplier will have some advice on energy efficiency for businesses, although if you want to be cynical about this, you may want to ask why a company that makes its money on selling energy wants to help you reduce your energy use. Organisations like the Carbon Trust also provide advisory and other services, but like most things in life, you may need to pay for specific information. As mentioned in Chapter 3, product and service suppliers will generally offer you free information about their offerings, as well as some general information that favour their particular offers.

Some may even offer you a free initial audit or assessment, but you know somewhere down the line you will be expected to pay them if you want to get useful and meaningful details.

Well, there is nothing wrong in paying if the advice, useful service or products help your organisation to go forward. However, you need to make sure it is the right technology for you currently; in the middle-distance future or in the long term.

There are four questions to ask yourself about technology, as shown in Figure 4.13.

Question 1 Can my current technology be improved?

Generally, the answer is yes; there is always the cutting edge to go for. However, the cutting edge can be more expensive, sometimes less tested and often not suited to your real needs. To explore this, you need to think BATNEEC – Best Available Technique/Technology Not Entailing Excessive Costs.[12] In other words, if you cannot really afford or justify it, then it is a not the right choice for you.

Whether it is improvable is really a matter of whether the current technology is delivering the value you require effectively and efficiently. This is where subjective feelings need to be balanced with objective data and information.

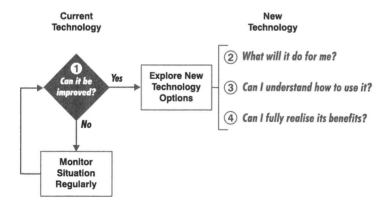

Figure 4.13 The Four Questions to Ask about Technology.

Another reason you may wish to replace technology is obsolescence. Sometimes, the trusty old equipment you had for years should be allowed to retire to the recycling pastures.[13] In these instances, the performance, and therefore the value, can be improved readily by more up-to-date technology or technologies that conform to the current legislative requirements. Legislation is often a driver for technology replacement. However, legislation can also be a minimum barrier where people invest at the lowest level that allows compliance. In these instances, although the performance may not be optimised, these decisions may be made on the basis of cash flow and cash in hand rather than performance or energy efficiency.

And if the answer to Question 1 is yes, then ask the next three questions about any new technology being explored. If the answer is no, then you need to set up some form of regular monitoring of your existing technology with regard to its effectiveness, efficiency and also its ongoing maintenance costs.

Question 2 What will it do for me?

This is a very important question because we do get bedazzled with technology: "Look at all the gleaming buttons!" We may become enamoured by a marketing message – "This will make you fitter, luckier and more successful!" and somehow forget that in some instances, a simpler[14] technology, or even the existing technology, will do the job just as well.

Understanding what the technology will do for you can be analysed in a more structured way by using the Balanced Scorecard methodology and by asking What and How:

- What will this technology do to benefit our finances/customers/staff/ processes, respectively?
- And How will we achieve the gains in each of these four areas?

If you do not understand what the technology will do for you, you are unlikely to be able to answer these questions in any meaningful way. Should you need to evaluate more than one type of technology, then score each answer from the What/How analysis and compare scores.

Question 3 Can I understand how to use it?

I have to admit, like many people, I have always found the buttons and functions on my video recorder somewhat baffling. This has since been extended to my phone, and also to many of the functions of the word processor I am using to write this. But if we invest in new technology for our organisation, we really need to make sure we can understand how to use it – and ideally use all that the technology has to offer. Technology investments at work, however, are unlike word processors, phones and video recorders where you can get a teenage relative to sort it out for you. You really do need to understand your technology investments. This relationship between you and your technology choice is shown in Figure 4.14.

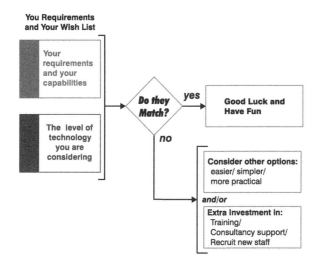

Figure 4.14 Matching Requirements and Technology.

Question 4 Can I get the full benefits of the technology?

This is the BIG question!

If you are not sure it will do the job for you, and are also not sure that you understand how to use it, then there's a very good chance that you are unlikely to get the full benefits without further investment. Again, by using the Balanced Scorecard and What/How techniques, you should be able to answer this question satisfactorily.

- What are the full benefits I can get in terms of finance/customers/staff/processes?
- And How are these benefits measured?

The difficulty in answering these questions is in the value you are receiving from the technology investment. Often, it is not easy to be absolutely sure whether you are getting any benefits, let alone getting the full benefits.

Let me use an example to illustrate this from a conversion I had with my wife earlier in 2016.

ME: Let's get a new super TV with curve screen and ultra high resolution, and all the other three- and four-letter acronyms that I can't pronounce! We can afford it, I think.

SHE: What will we watch on this new TV then?

ME: We can watch animal programmes, nature stuff – really good on high resolution.

SHE: We don't watch nature programmes.
ME: Hmm, we can watch sports then; it's really great on high definition.
SHE: I don't watch sports.
ME: Aah, we can watch the news then.
SHE: You want a super TV just to watch the news?[15]

Example Summary: the Four Questions and the Answers.

1   Can we improve on our first-generation flat-screen TV? Yes
2   What will it do for me? Not a lot more than the old set
3   Can I understand how to use it? Not really, can't understand the acronyms
4   Can I fully realise its benefits? Probably not, but look at how nice and shiny it is...

Improvement for improvement sake is not necessarily an optimal option, even if someone else is paying for it – if you cannot make the best use of the technology, then it becomes a waste – of your time and efforts, as well as Systems Energy being used ineffectively.

Dealing with people

The third element of Everyday Sustainability is people and their behaviour. Organisations are full of people with a range of opinions towards environmental responsibility. They can be fanatic, keen supporters to indifferent, withdrawn and vehemently opposing. These are your colleagues and also the people you want to gain support for your energy efficiency proposal. Remember, however, that they all have their own reasons to be at work, and probably not all of them have effective use of energy as their prime objective. The fanatic and the totally negative can be left alone for the moment, as you probably can't tone down the former, and you'll probably never shift the latter, so we end up dealing with the rest of the gang.

The approach I am proposing is pragmatic on how to engage the individuals in the team. Basically, you work with whatever people you have available to you.

• Make sure those who are not too engaged are directed to do this or that with sanctions for non-compliance;
• The vaguely engaged ones are shown how to get more out of the initiative;
• Encouragements for those who are not too sure; and delegation for the keen ones.[16]

As for the totally negative people, I reckon they may need to be isolated to prevent them from undermining your initiative. It is unfortunate, but there is a point to the somewhat harsh saying "my way or the highway." You cannot allow individuals to block your path towards more effective use of energy, and with it, your contribution towards global sustainability. Now, not every organisation can take the stark my way/highway approach, since it is likely to contravene corporate rules (or legislation), but you need to make it clear that if the individual is not going to support the corporate strategy, then his/her future in the organisation may be limited.

My suggestions for segmenting the workforce are summarised in Figure 4.15 and Table 4.4. You may find these classifications a bit too detailed or not suitable for your organisation. As this is a generic set, I am sure you can establish a similar set that reflects your organisation better.

What if you are in the public sector and have perhaps less flexibility in sanctioning people for non-compliance? My suggestion for your consideration is

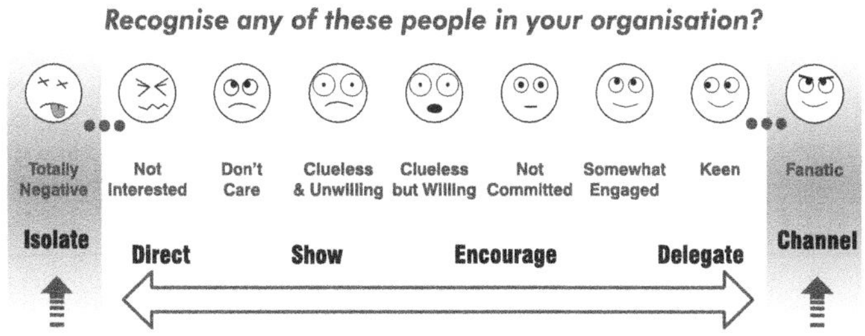

Recognise any of these people in your organisation?

| Totally Negative | Not Interested | Don't Care | Clueless & Unwilling | Clueless but Willing | Not Committed | Somewhat Engaged | Keen | Fanatic |

Isolate **Direct** **Show** **Encourage** **Delegate** **Channel**

Figure 4.15 Working with a Spectrum of Behaviour.

Table 4.4 Behaviour and Engagement

Behaviour Trait	Suggested Ways to Engage These Individuals
Totally negative	Isolate people who may damage your initiative by spreading rumour or misinformation. Perhaps you can set them a detailed research project on mid- to long-term corporate risks – it should get them out of your hair for a while. If this person is a valued prima donna, then the approach needs to be completely different (see the next section).
Not interested	Find out why they are not interested, and try to market your promotional/inspiration themes to include an area of their interest. If they have no areas of interest that can be engaged, then tell them being efficient is part of their job.
Don't care	If people don't care about the initiative, then make it fun for them to do by linking it to an area they care about (staying employed, for example) and recognise their efforts.
Clueless & unwilling	Train them with the necessary knowledge and context, and then reclassify their trait.
Clueless but willing	Train them with the necessary knowledge and context, then get them involved in the activities. Always recognise their efforts.

(Continued)

Behaviour Trait	Suggested Ways to Engage These Individuals
Not committed	Find out what rings their bell – what incentives do they need to get involved? Then explore (and negotiate) those incentives with them. Otherwise, just put them in a position where they cannot do a lot of damage, but also allow them to achieve success in the initiative to motivate them. Always recognise the efforts they put in.
Somewhat engaged	Let these people try with your encouragement and support, if needed. Make sure they understand that failure is not the end of the world. Recognise their efforts and celebrate success.
Keen	Ask these people what they think will help the initiative to succeed, and then support them in their actions. Celebrate success.
Fanatic	Channel – you cannot direct this person because s/he probably knows more about it than you do. Channelling their enthusiasm is a good way to keep them engaged and allow you to keep control. Losing control of the fanatic is probably as problematic as having a rejectionist slagging off your initiative.

to use political correctness as part of your toolkit: Very few people want the (polite but politically correct) public ostracism that comes with being against sustainability.

What about prima donnas?

Prima donnas are an unavoidable part of many organisations. Dictionaries usually define them as people who think they are better than everyone else around them and who do not always work well in a team. If they only *think* they are better than everyone else, then they can be classified into one of the above segments; but if they are really better than everyone else, then you may have a bit of a problem on your hands. Some of the reasons they are being negative are understandable. After all, if your prima donna thinks s/he is really the best thing since sliced bread, then s/he probably thinks it is beneath her/him to review boring process parameters and help dull colleagues to reduce waste (Figure 4.16). I mean, they're here to save the world, not to do the donkey work...

Hey! Wait a minute, this is about saving the world (too) and your prima donna can show off how wonderful they are at the same time as helping you. I believe that, basically, prima donnas are often vain, and you can always try to engage (or manipulate) them through their ego. Tell them that only their towering reputation can make the sustainability initiative a success, but they need to be seen to be humble, as that's how sustainability is done.

If they still refuse to be engaged and they are bringing in 45 per cent of your corporate income, then either make them a director (and let them get

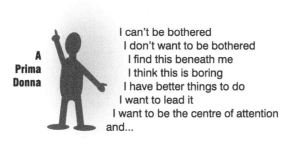

Figure 4.16 Some Reasons for Being Negative.

on with what they do uniquely) or get them away from you by putting them on a special project where they can nurture their ego.

I have now gone through the preparations for an Everyday Sustainability campaign. The next few chapters talk about making it happen.

Notes

1 Six Sigma Quality and Lean Operations are both tool frameworks. These and other improvement techniques are described in Appendix 2.
2 This is a Lean Operations term that describes how value is added in a process. See Appendix 2 for more information.
3 Hidden because we don't see them shown in the Value Stream Map.
4 Walking the process isn't necessarily just physically walking, but instead following the flow of the process through every step. It should include logging the workarounds, pointless activities as well as waiting, changes and materials and data flow.
5 Lean Operations is against working in batches, as batching can hide ineffectiveness in the process. However, as anyone doing mass mailings will tell you – you don't send junk mail one piece at a time, you take them to the post office in large bags!
6 SIPOC is a Six Sigma Quality tool and it is an acronym for Supplier-Inputs-Process-Outputs-Customer. Find out more in Appendix 2.
7 Described in Chapter 3, and see Appendix 2 for more information.
8 Apocryphal story: A family always baked its turkey with the drumsticks cut off. One day a guest asked "Why?" The answer was "Grandma always did it this way". So off to ask Grandma and she said, "Our first oven was too small to fit the whole turkey with legs on, so I cut them off".
9 *Gemba* – in Japanese, this means the real place – i.e. not in your head. It is Toyota's way of going to where it is happening, see it for real and collect real data. This is opposite to sitting at one's desk and guessing the problem and then guessing the solutions. This is described further in Appendix 2.
10 Despite it being a relatively common management tool, it was included as part of the Seven New Management and Planning Tools in Japanese quality management (1976). The tools in this group were not new, but their bundling into a coherent package for analysis was new for its time; see Appendix 2 for more details.

11   Failure Modes and Effects Analysis originally came from a US Military Speci-
     fication (perhaps accounting for the lack of an easy-on-the-tongue acronym…).
     This is a straightforward risk assessment procedure with the extra element of
     detectability. See Appendix 2 for more information.
12   Best Available Technology Not Exceeding Excessive Costs. BATNEEC is part
     of the European Union directive on pollution in 1984. Sometimes, "technique"
     is replaced by "technology" in BATNEEC.
13   According to *The Economist* (19 May 2017), the current revival of vinyl records is
     slowed by the lack of up-to-date production machinery to press the records – the
     old ones were scrapped (and their producers closed) with the introduction of the
     CD in the early 1990s.
14   This is not necessarily a generalisation, but new technology is often less simple
     because there is a need to justify all the gleaming buttons – they all have to do
     something, whether useful or not….
15   We did end up buying one, and I can now watch YouTube kitten videos on it….
16   Some of you will have recognised this as being adapted from *The One Minute
     Manager* by Blanchard.

5   Conducting an energy-use audit

To get moving on Everyday Sustainability, you need to find out, first, whether your activities at work are adding value, enabling value or creating waste; and second, to find out whether energy is used effectively and efficiently. This is part of exploring energy use issues and uses the DMAIC[1] (Define, Measure, Analyse, Improve and Control) methodology, as shown in Figure 5.1.

Identifying assets

The audit starts by identifying the available assets and how they use Operational and Systems Energy, respectively. This energy-use audit is not necessarily about process management, but instead about process issues relating directly to energy use. This can include, for example, dirty overhead light reflectors, poorly maintained equipment as well as equipment left on for no apparent reason.

Luckily, it is not particularly hard to find out what energy is used by both large pieces of plant and overheads. Virtually all equipment comes with some power use documentation, and it is a matter of looking up the specifications (or checking the label on the equipment) to find out about the amount of energy used. The availability of clamp or plug-in meters, like the examples shown in Figure 5.2, make it very easy to check how much energy is being used by specific pieces of equipment.

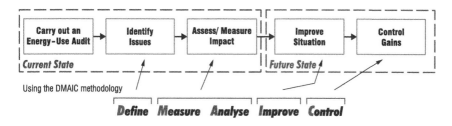

Figure 5.1 Energy-Use Audit – Dealing with Issues.

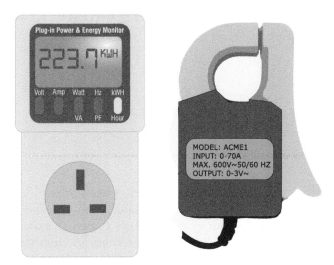

Figure 5.2 Plug-In/Portable Energy Monitoring Submeters.

Before carrying out an audit, it is prudent to define the process perimeter of the selected area of audit. Within an organisation's workspace, it is possible to have processes spanning different locations. You need to decide where the perimeters are and that you are not arbitrarily breaking up a process just because they are not in adjacent locations.

Then come the boring bits: Identify and list all the power using equipment and/or services in the selected location. This requires some diligence, and probably overalls and gloves too, as there may be some crawling around floors, heights and narrow spaces.[2] You will need to list what the particular equipment or services are, their location and their energy use values. There may also be a need to check the actual power consumption with the portable metering equipment to make sure you get an acceptable level of accuracy.

It is possible that some equipment and plant may have fluctuating power usage and demand patterns, and others may have a history of non-standard usage. These also need to be reviewed and recorded so that your power use values are reflecting the day-to-day reality of your organisation. (And yes, I know, it is tedious.)

You will also need to collect sufficient information so that you have some confidence in the data you are collecting. This means relying on a single reading is not a good idea for major plant and equipment, however, for items such as desktop computers, an approximation of the average hours used and the number of units in the location is likely to be sufficient.[3] Once the initial data set is established, equipment changes can be readily accommodated with less effort.

With all the information gathered, you can then calculate the overall energy used, total Operational Energy used and total Systems Energy used. You may also wish to check your utility bills for fuel types and thence segment the energy use by fuel types. This provides you with a point of reference; you then need to decide what interval you should use to repeat the measurements. The interval should correspond to your work patterns, or if relevant, months or quarters.

Figure 5.3 shows this process as an overview flow diagram. You may have other procedures for carrying out an energy audit, and the Internet has quite a number of templates you can explore too.

The initial energy use data forms the baseline for improvements and the Energy Productivity audit can help to identify potential issues, whether Operational or Systems. Once these are analysed, you can carry out an improvement action or programme aimed at the infrastructure of your organisation. The core of this, like any other DMAIC problem-solving exercise, is to gather sufficient information such that useful decisions can be taken. However, unlike process improvement actions, the data gathering has a significant technical element in terms of how the plant and fittings are performing, as well as looking through maintenance and operations logs, respectively, for details. Figure 5.4 shows a suggested procedure for improving the corporate infrastructure of plant, equipment and fittings.

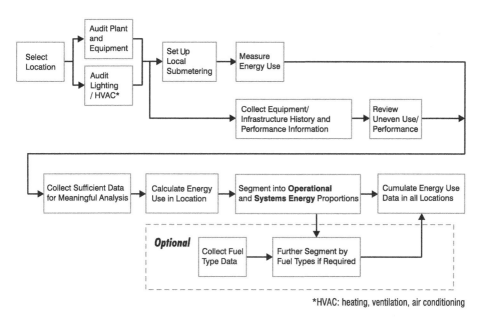

*HVAC: heating, ventilation, air conditioning

Figure 5.3 Energy-Use Audit Process.

Energy Use Audit

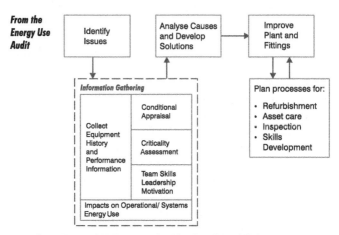

Source: Elements of this diagram are adapted from Peter Willmott & SA Partners

Figure 5.4 Infrastructure (Plant, Equipment and Fittings) Improvement.

Asset care

Asset care is a major element in this improvement action. This has four main elements, as detailed below.

Historical Performance Data: This is to identify any pattern of problems, for example:

- Machinery or equipment that never really worked right since installation;
- Equipment that has a history of minor problems and stoppages; or
- Plant that needed a long time to settle down to a steady state level of performance.

Conditional Appraisal: This is a visual assessment of the physical state of the equipment, plant or fitting; for example:

- A broken control panel;
- Fluorescent lights with dirty reflectors and housing;
- Plant or equipment that is leaking lubricant; or
- Equipment with accumulated dirt that hinders performance.

Criticality Assessment: This assesses the elements that may have contributed to the performance and/or the condition of the equipment. Generally, the cause is likely to be inadequacy in one or more of the following: manufacture, installation, use and maintenance. In addition, malfunction is also a likely prospect for heavily used plant and equipment.[4]

Team Skills/Leadership/Motivation: This is the people element of the infrastructure.

- Team skills: Does the staff know how to use the equipment/plant? Does the maintenance team have the necessary knowledge and skills to deal with any issues?
- Leadership: Do leaders in both the maintenance team and the user team encourage effective asset care and lead by example?
- Motivation: Do users report arising issues before they become catastrophes? Do maintenance team members carry out general problem spotting/visual monitoring when they are on other jobs? Is the maintenance team respected?

Impacts on the Operational and Systems Energy Use, respectively: This is the crucial point in this analysis. How much impact is the problem causing? Since it is likely you will have more than one problem arising at the same time, then this assessment will help to prioritise your resources.

The five elements described above all contribute to issues within the infrastructure, and while some of these are linked to process improvement, many are about asset management only. Nonetheless, asset management contributes to effective Value Enabling and therefore should be treated with some priority. The improvement actions can include, for example:

- **Refurbishment/Renewal**: If the organisation is in constant firefighting mode, then routine activities such as refurbishment can slip away from focus.
- **Asset Care**: If there is no budget to refurbish or replace old equipment, then a more rigorous asset care regime is needed to make sure everything works until the budget is available. An asset care strategy is also something to consider if your organisation relies on its equipment to deliver customer value.
- **Inspection**: This should be part of the asset care strategy, with both formal inspections and daily inspections; and reporting of problems arising by the team working in that location.
- **Skills Development**: This is to ensure the users, maintenance team and decision makers (or specifiers) have sufficient skills and knowledge to choose, use and maintain the assets for the organisation.

To summarise all the above, I would suggest the acronym: BATNEEC.[5] Remember, if you can't afford it, don't buy it. And "afford" includes: the capital purchase cost, the costs of training your people to use and maintain the purchase and whether the purchase delivers better value than the existing assets.

Water

Water is treated by many energy management professionals as an energy resource, and it can similarly be divided into Operational Water use and Systems Water use. The audit is therefore similar to those described in this chapter. You will need monitoring equipment like ultrasonic flow meters, which are non-invasive and clamp onto the water flow pipes. This type of equipment does not interrupt the process and therefore has no downtime cost implications.

Maintenance – does it matter?

Why am I so bothered about maintenance? Because it is a hidden leak of value in your organisation. Poor maintenance means your assets (which you paid for or are still paying for) will not deliver their full value to you. Examining this with Overall Effectiveness analysis shows that poorly maintained assets may break down more frequently and therefore hammer your Availability Key Performance Indicator (KPI), then there are assets that are not working properly, which can slow down your process leading to a hammering of your Performance KPI; and if the assets are not working properly, output tolerances may slip beyond specified limits and so hammer your Quality KPI.

The evolution of maintenance usually starts with catastrophic maintenance.[6] This is maintenance that only happens when something is wrong, and it is a high-risk option. Evolving from this is scheduled or planned maintenance. This conjures an image of summer factory shutdowns, but it is also used in lifecycle maintenance where the effective lifetime of a component is taken into account and replaced when it comes up to a certain amount of usage.[7]

With modern electronic sensors and IT storage capacity being more and more affordable, continuous condition monitoring allows a more flexible level of maintenance where potential problems are spotted and dealt with before they become catastrophes.[8]

Total Productive Maintenance, TPM,[9] is a modern approach to maintenance that takes condition monitoring to both the users and the maintenance team. The users carry out daily "clean up," which becomes a minor inspection, and they also undertake minor maintenance and asset care, as well as giving the maintenance team a "heads up" on issues arising.

My colleague Peter Willmott of SA Partners, a consultancy, tells me that the impact of poor maintenance is essentially sixfold. This is known as the Six Major Losses, shown in Figure 5.5. Although the Six Major Losses come from engineering and manufacturing industries, they are equally relevant and applicable for service/office environment.

- **Equipment Breakdown** – When the equipment (or people) is not working, not a lot will happen.
- **Adjustments** – When you are fiddling with the various settings (or sorting out your workspace), not a lot will happen too.

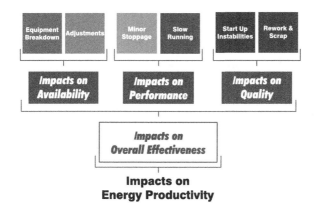

Figure 5.5 The Six Major Losses and their Impacts.

- **Minor Stoppages** – Well, if you are off having a cup of coffee (and the equipment is doing its equivalent of having a break, for example stoppage caused by overheating) you will not be performing at the designed pace.
- **Slow Running** – The title says it all; poor maintenance (or a lack of sleep) may mean you cannot get it going at full speed safely.
- **Start-Up Instabilities** – I think people can relate to this as the Monday morning feeling (or just the morning feeling!); the thing is like old-fashioned neon lights flashing a few times before settling down, or your omelette pan not doing so well until it reaches a good temperature. Either way, the output will not necessarily meet the specifications.
- **Rework and Scrap** – If you or your equipment are not doing well, chances are that the output is likely to have errors and defects.

The impact of poor maintenance can be profound in how it affects Energy Productivity. Since your assets are not optimised for delivering or enabling value, then there is no way you are getting the most from the energy you are using. Maintenance matters because it affects every aspect of Overall Effectiveness. You cannot deliver your products and services as designed if your Availability is lowered. This then compromises Performance, because it does not matter how hard you try, it is not easy to reach the designed pace in your Performance since you have fewer assets available to deliver the planned outcomes. Quality defect is not just scratches, blemishes or smudged ink; not being on time is also a quality defect to a customer.

Figure 5.6 shows how this impact is multiplied by the progressive reduction of resources to do the work. Essentially, poor asset maintenance reduces our capacity to deliver value, but not necessarily without reducing our energy use. This means a double lot of hammering and increased waste all around, as shown on Figure 5.6. So yes, maintenance matters; even if it is not in the headlines, it matters to the bottom line.

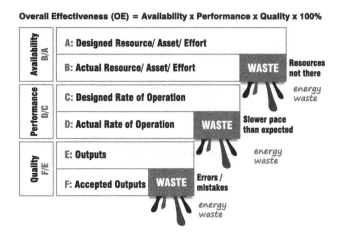

Figure 5.6 How Waste Reduces the Overall Effectiveness.

How Facilities Management (FM) can help reduce energy waste

FM (Facilities Management) is often described as the efficient and effective delivery of support services to an organisation. In other words, it is often about Enabling Value. Many organisations subcontract these support activities to save money and to gain the capability of companies specialising in one or more particular aspect of FM. Nonetheless, FM is usually thought of as working in the built environment: from cleaning the office to fixing the air conditioning.

To me, FM is the equally essential cousin of maintenance, because FM plays an important role in Energy Productivity and sustainability. Why do I say that? Well, it is because the FM colleagues can act as an organisation's early warning network, alerting us to potential problems, especially in the Systems Energy side. The FM team is more or less everywhere in the physical workplace, often at the hours when we are not. So they get to see the workplace not cluttered, and, more importantly, they see it without the Hidden Waste baggage that we have. This means they can spot things that we pass over. Furthermore, because their duties relate to the physical workspace, they often pay more attention to it than we do.

The question is, however, what do they do with this information? Is there a way for this information to get to us so that we can do something about it?

Now we come to some of the practical difficulties in engaging the FM team as a partner in doing sustainability. First, they are involved in value-enabling activities, and, as such, they do not have a loud voice in the income-generating areas of an organisation. Second, the FM team is often viewed as being low in an organisation's pecking order and therefore as a function not too well respected.[10] Third, they are often contracted to an outside body, which further distances them from the corporate decision-making team.

Because of the type of work being carried out, sometimes the FM team members do not necessarily get the respect they should receive. Some of them also are perhaps migrant workers with a weaker grasp of the language spoken in the organisation.

Beyond this range of barriers, there is also low pay, low morale and perhaps poor leadership. It does not take a lot for the FM team members to forget to tell us that the building management system may be on the blink, as the building is rather warm late in the evening. They may also miss reporting that a sink in the third floor toilet is leaking. How do we engage them to tell us or tell a relevant leader in our organisation or in their hierarchy? Is there a procedure for quick action, or is it going to take forever and involve going up their own chain-of-command to their own client manager who then tells your contract manager a few days later?

Does your organisation have a process that encourages direct communications and reporting? If there is, then that's great; you can further encourage them by inviting them to a short discussion every month to explore issues they noticed and also their suggestions for improvements in their working realm. If you want them to report on energy waste, then you need to give them a short bit of training on spotting energy waste, as well as making it easy for them to report it.

If there isn't, then you should think about how to get the most from this resource too. To engage people effectively, you need to think about what's really in it for them to let you know of such issues. It is definitely a case of carrots and not sticks.[11]

Providing some waste-spotting training for the FM team is a win-win scenario. You need to make sure the training content makes sense to the people involved and that the information allows them to make the right decisions.

My recommendation – show respect to the FM teams: Make sure the training and meeting for the FM team takes place in paid time; many organisations ask the FM team to come early or stay late, but unpaid. They will come, as they value their jobs and because your organisation is the customer, but there will be resentment and they probably won't pay a lot of attention. I know I wouldn't.

Examples of other early warning systems

I mentioned earlier that FM can act as an early warning system for your organisation, because it can provide a "heads up" on potential problems. Another way to have an early warning is to model the system and then explore things that can go wrong. Just like the Swim Lanes in Chapter 4 and the Designing out Waste in Chapter 1,[12] modern technology can help us by providing a detailed modelling of the workplace. For example, the Building

Information Modelling (BIM)[13] approach lets the building designers create a virtual model of how the building is structured, with details on how the different bits can be put together. This type of detailed modelling can readily help the building operators (especially the FM and maintenance teams) to explore their particular working environment and ensure that the working methods of these teams are optimised for the specific building.

Furthermore, the development of Virtual Reality (VR) software means that it is possible for maintenance teams to be trained in a virtual working environment. This can provide significant opportunities to improve the maintenance processes and procedures, resulting in safer and cheaper operations.

Systems like BIM help the designers to ensure that the workspace is optimised in design and layout for the users, but what about the equipment? Often the building operators cannot get the best out of their modern complex buildings because they were neither party to the design of the building nor its construction. A methodology called Soft Landings,[14] according to my colleague Isabelle Beaumont of Workplace Futures, offers a strategic approach to enable not just a building's owner to get a well-scoped brief of the equipment in plain English before handover, but also smoother commissioning, handover and transition to user processes. The benefits of such early information mean that the building operators can compare the as-designed energy use with the in-occupation data and therefore optimise the energy use of the building.

We have now touched on "data" – the objective of audits and the basis on which decisions are made, so let's explore the relationship we have with data in Everyday Sustainability.

Data: measuring, collecting and what else?

Data is a mesmerising word. Besides the pedantic argument about singular and plural forms, it is also big business, or do I mean Big Data? Is it open, shared or closed? Whatever it is, there is a lot of hype and jargon involved. My intention for this book is straightforward; we are dealing with improving the way we work to enhance the organisation's Everyday Sustainability. While this is a straightforward aim, is managing data really as simple as that? Unfortunately not; I reckon data takes a fairly serendipitous path through our lives, as shown in Figure 5.7. While the picture is a light-hearted look, the underlying intent is quite serious, so let's have a more detailed exploration.

"Stuff" is out there: on the Internet, in some databases, in a published book, on a library shelf. But to you and me initially, it's random and unorganised. So we need to collect what we want from the "stuff" so that we can use it. Collecting is basically two steps: setting search criteria and then establishing retrieval methods.

To set the criteria, we need to ask what it is that we want to look for. Is it the surface data or any underlying data? Figure 5.8 highlights how such an enquiry may appear. This is a form of a Tree Diagram.[15] From Figure 5.8, the two further questions can each/both be applied to the secondary questions individually to provide a fuller picture.

a light-hearted look

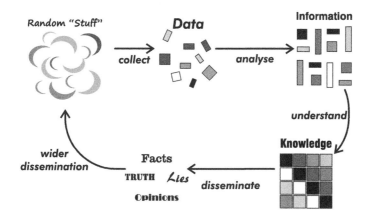

Figure 5.7 Data – An Evolutionary Cycle.

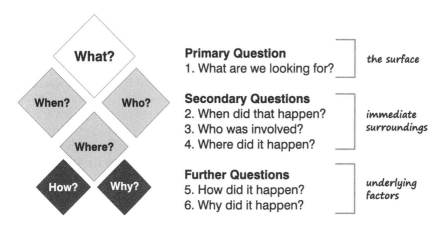

Figure 5.8 Setting a Search Criteria.

For example, if we are to measure the effectiveness of a process, do we just look at the Availability, Performance and Quality information, or do we also explore the underlying factors that contribute to the individual effectiveness components? Once we agree on the criteria, it is time to explore the way the data is gathered. Here we need some guidelines or rules to help us because otherwise we can end up with chaos, useless data or wrong data.

First, set our target: Are we really gathering what we set out to collect? Are we collecting the wrong things instead of the right things?

Are we focussing on what we really want to find out? Are we *only* measuring what we set out to measure and not everything that we can find? And even worse, are we finding out things we never really wanted to find out in the first place? The latter case is something that can burn through a tremendous amount of time; a good example is surfing the Internet and clicking on what appears to be interesting and sort of related.[16] Also, we need to make sure that someone will actually want to use the data we collect. Therefore, we need some experience when we design the gathering process to make sure we stick to the target.

Another area to pay attention to is whether we have the knowledge to interpret the data gathered. This is a factor that sometimes results in people building very complex models to explain the results they gathered.[17]

Now we get to the core of the data collecting: Is our method the right way to gather the information we need? Do we need to go and talk to people or would desktop research do? Should we go to where the action is (*gemba*) or can we find it in a report? We need to make sure that the value of the data is worth the cost of gathering it. It is nice to get a field trip to Paris to gather data of the city's layout, but sometimes a street map may do just as well.

The next item to note is that we may need a data gathering methodology that is not just simple, easy and practical but also allows consistent results no matter who gathers the data. This is critically important, because if everyone has their own way of gathering the data, the lack of consistency may render the information useless. (In quality jargon, this is known as variation – a bane to all quality management professionals.)

Inconsistency in gathering the data can often be addressed by a standardised method. However, if the physical access to capturing the data is difficult or dangerous, then a standard method may not be able to overcome the inconsistent measurements. Imagine taking readings from an electricity meter in a very confined space that is hot and dark. The discomfort and contortions may impact the data gathering. In these instances, access to the data gathering can readily affect the quality of the data gathered. An alternative is to use systems like BIM to design out hot, dark or confined working spaces where possible to eliminate this type of variation in measurements.

We have defined the search criteria, worked out the ways we want to gather the data and now we have the data. The question then becomes one of whether we can analyse this data so that it is useful to us within whatever timetable we have. For example, your amateur dramatics club is hosting in a one-week run of a play. Something didn't go right in the final rehearsal, and you were asked to fix it. You have a short period of time to gather data and come up with a solution. Say you managed to gather the data during the final rehearsal itself, but then it took you two weeks to come up with a solution. In such instances, the solution cannot help solve the problem within the allotted time and therefore is fairly useless.

Following analysis and understanding, we now have knowledge, and we can now think about disseminating it to other people (or in plain English, tell people). In Figure 5.7, I light-heartedly suggested that when we disseminate data, it becomes several things:

- Facts – the details (but can sometimes be boring)
- Truth – what I tell you
- Lies – what other people tell you
- Opinions – from people we are not too bothered about

Nowadays, the amount of fake news means that we are encountering more and more information that needs to be classified in one of these four categories. These classifications, unfortunately, can contribute to uncertainty if we are not careful with our information dissemination. What should you do? Simple: Believe me, of course, since I am telling you the truth!

Seriously, what *should* we do with the knowledge and information? In the real world, the policy of how to disseminate information should be a major corporate decision. On the one hand, the good practice arising from doing Everyday Sustainability should be shared so everyone can benefit. However, the good practices are also your competitive advantage, so you cannot really share that. To untangle this, we need to explore the nature of data: whether it is open, shared or closed as shown in Figure 5.9.

Everyday Sustainability activities can provide a large quantity of information, with the Energy Productivity KPI at the top of the stack. This should

Open Data
Data that anyone can share, use or access

Shared Data
Data that has access criteria:
Named access – data shared only
with named people or organisations
Attribute-based access – data available
to specific defined groups
Public access – data available to anyone

Closed Data
Data that is only accessible by the owner, people
and teams within the organisation or by people
specifically permitted by the owner

Source: some of the contents are adapted from the Open Data Institute

Figure 5.9 The Three Types of Data.

be open and shared with everyone, as it is a headline figure and gives away nothing except how well your organisation is doing.

Immediately below this is the information on how the Energy Productivity KPI is achieved. This can include the various Overall Effectiveness parameters, as well as outlines of projects and activities together with summaries of knowledge gained. This information is the sort of stuff you share with business partners, as well as selected members of your supply chain, and customers. The disclosure to the supply chain can encourages them to improve their performance and disclosure to customers to enhance their confidence in your organisation.[18]

Special interest groups, such as industry-specific groups, researchers and perhaps government agencies, can also fit into the Shared Data category, although you may wish to have some restrictions on what is disclosed. For example, a case study by a government agency is generally welcomed, but let's be honest, you will disclose general overviews and hardly any specific details.

Finally, we come to the good stuff; the details about what you did to enhance your Energy Productivity KPI. This kind of information is for staff and other people who signed a non-disclosure agreement, since these details provide your competitive edge. This general classification is shown in Figure 5.10.

There is a school of thought that suggests that there is no reason why you should not disclose more details about your operational activities or processes. It goes something like this: Be open and tell people what you are doing. It will take them some time to work it out and get going, but they will never be able to replicate the process, because your process is based on how you use technology and how your people work to deliver Everyday Sustainability – both of which are unique to your organisation. Furthermore, by the time

Data	Data examples	Shared with
OPEN	Energy Productivity KPI	*everyone*
SHARED	General Principles of Overall Effectiveness Outline of projects and activities Summaries of knowledge gained	*business partners, suppliers, customers, special interest groups*
CLOSED	Details about projects and activities Details about knowledge gained	*staff and others who signed non-disclosure agreements*

Figure 5.10 Managing the Data from Everyday Sustainability Activities.

your competitors figure this out, you are again ahead by a long way because you are practising continuous improvement.

After all this, what about sharing good sustainability practice then? My suggestion is to share just the principles and generic methodologies, or instead, get them to buy this book.

Notes

1 DMAIC is a Six Sigma Quality technique explored further in Chapter 6 and Appendix 2.
2 Always comply with your organisation's Health and Safety rules.
3 Except when you have heavy-duty graphics cards or workstations where the power requirements can be up to 600 W per station.
4 Generally, this happens when the warranty runs out!
5 A good basis for the purchase decision is the BATNEEC approach; see Chapter 4 for more details.
6 This is enshrined in conventional thinking as "If it ain't broke, don't fix it."
7 This happens in car service and aircraft components.
8 For example, Formula 1 racing cars have sensors reporting slow punctures during the race. Similarly, many Enterprise Information Systems will report problems in the processes.
9 See Appendix 2 for more information.
10 This low-ish respect does not apply to the FM team's individuals, but to the function overall.
11 Sticks or sanctions won't work since a threatened individual can always say "I didn't see it" or "It wasn't happening when I went by" – nobody wins when this happens.
12 Remember the Waste Hierarchy?
13 For more information, search for BIM on the Internet.
14 In the UK, there are two somewhat different versions: Soft Landings and Government Soft Landings – look them up on the Internet for more information.
15 This was explored in Chapter 4; see Appendix 2 for more details.
16 Remember: Safe surfing means you use both common sense and deploy relevant up-to-date security tools.
17 Disclosure: I proposed some models of atomic diffusion in my PhD thesis based on my experimental results. Was I right? Who knows? Anyway, I got my doctorate.
18 For example, British Airways (BA) runs open days to selected people on their frequent flyer programmes where you can tour the service hangers, sit on new planes, get free ice cream and all-in-all realise what a nice bunch of people BA's staff are.

6   The analysis

Problems and solutions

Now that you have gathered a lot of information about your processes, your technology and your teams, we turn our attention to the type of issues you might have spotted and then explore ways to deal with them. Some of these may appear to be quite simple problems, but we need to make sure that any hidden causes are identified and dealt with. Once again, we will use both Lean Operations and Six Sigma Quality methods and techniques to analyse and resolve these problems.

To start, we need to remember some fundamentals about waste in general and energy waste in particular:

- Virtually all economic activities cause some form of environmental impact
  And
- All economic activities require energy

To minimise the environmental impacts from our activities, we need to make sure our economic activities, or work, are efficient and effective – in other words, we need to minimise waste. This was outlined through a process analysis in Figure 2.3, but described in a more activity-focussed way in Figure 6.1.

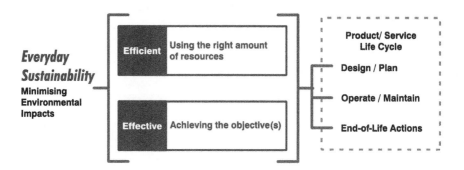

Figure 6.1 Everyday Sustainability – Getting There.

Our focus here is to improve the Energy Productivity Key Performance Indicator (KPI) through Everyday Sustainability, or, cut out waste in everything we do. The concept of being both effective in *what we do* and efficient in *how we do it* is the precursor to process improvement. There are many ways to carry out an improvement programme; a generic model is shown in Figure 6.2. To start, you (or your organisation) will need to establish some commitment towards improvement and from there, a strategy to go forward.

Management frameworks for analysis

The strategy should be linked to an overall plan for improving Energy Productivity: gathering process information as well as top-level customer needs. You can develop the strategy using a framework such as the Balanced Scorecard (see Appendix 2 on how to do this) or the Triple Bottom Line (see Appendix 2). These tool frameworks make the job easier by helping you divide the objectives into relevant strategic areas, as shown in Table 6.1.

The focus on each area can then be assessed with simple tools like the Strengths Weaknesses Opportunities Threats (SWOT) analysis (see Appendix 2). The strengths and weaknesses assessment allows the organisation to understand what it is good at doing and to fix what it is less

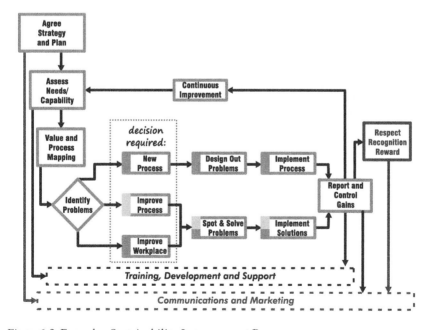

Figure 6.2 Everyday Sustainability Improvement Process.

Table 6.1 Strategic Management Frameworks

Balanced Scorecard Perspectives	Triple Bottom Line Areas
Economic/finance	Profit: economic/finance
Customer	People: social
Staff	Planet: environmental
Processes	

Table 6.2 Example of Using the Balanced Scorecard and SWOT Analysis

Balanced Scorecard perspectives	What are our **Strengths** in these individual areas?	What **Opportunities** can we exploit from our particular Strengths?	What are our **Weaknesses** in these individual areas?	What can **Threaten** our Weaknesses in these individual areas?
Economic/ finance				
Customer				
Staff				
Processes				

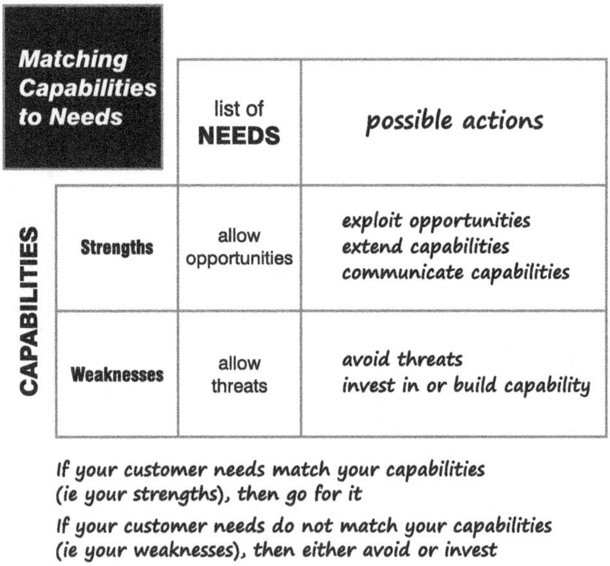

Matching Capabilities to Needs	list of **NEEDS**	*possible actions*
Strengths	allow opportunities	*exploit opportunities* *extend capabilities* *communicate capabilities*
Weaknesses	allow threats	*avoid threats* *invest in or build capability*

If your customer needs match your capabilities
(ie your strengths), then go for it

If your customer needs do not match your capabilities
(ie your weaknesses), then either avoid or invest

Figure 6.3 Matching Capabilities to Needs.

good at doing. Once this strategy and plan are agreed upon, then it is time to start the communications plan and work out effective ways of marketing the message (in this case, Everyday Sustainability) to different parts of the organisation. An example of this analysis with the Balanced Scorecard is shown in Table 6.2.

Having a strategic direction and an awareness of strengths/weaknesses, the organisation can then assess its operational level customer needs against the organisation's current capability to fulfil these particular needs. These needs and capabilities can be matched against your organisation's strengths and weaknesses, and from there, appropriate strategic directions can be chosen. This is shown in Figure 6.3.

With the direction, needs and capabilities being logged, it is time to see where value is being delivered in the operations and conversely, to identify problems, choke points and other areas where waste is occurring.

Looking for trouble

The current state Value Stream Map is a good starting point to look at both values and waste – where value delivery can be optimised and waste can be minimised. After an initial paper or computer-based analysis, it is time to do the *gemba* (see Footnote 9 in Chapter 4 and Appendix 2), and go to where it is all happening.

From walking the Value Stream, you are likely to spot some process hiccups or other activities that seem pointless or without value. In this chapter we go looking for all the potential and actual problems. These are identified, analysed and improvements are planned so that we can then develop a Future State Value Stream Map.

With a list of problems identified and an initial analysis completed, it is possible to segment these into three categories (see Figure 6.2):

- Design a **new process** (changes "what we do" to "do different things")
- Improve a **current process** (changes "what we do" to "do things differently")
- Improve the **current workplace** (physical reorganisation of the working environment)

Often workplace improvement is the cheapest option[1] in terms of investment as well as learning, with process improvement in the middle and new process being most expensive in terms of investment and learning.

End to end

With your Current State Value Stream Map in hand, it can be better to start the improvement analysis from the customer end, or the process end point. Why? Because it is closest to the customer, or end user, and any benefit will be immediately passed on to the people the process is designed for. This may seem counter-intuitive, but there is another major benefit from starting at the finish: You can quickly see whether any procedure or process step adds value.

Another reason for not starting the improvement analysis from the beginning of the process is that something fixed at the customer end may remove the need for some action at the starting end. Furthermore, you may end up improving something that does not necessarily benefit the customer or carrying out an improvement that may be of some local benefit but not for the entire process.

How is it possible for an improvement not to add value?

Improvement means increasing effectiveness, right? Not necessarily, because improvements can be *both* efficient *and* effective; therefore, an unnecessary step, however effective and well executed, is still a waste if it is not efficient.

The fundamental reason for a business process is to deliver value to the customer or end user.[2] Therefore, a customer-driven process should aim to be most efficient and effective. A supplier-driven process, on the other hand, is designed to suit the needs of the process operator. This can mean batching and creating inventories rather than having a just-in-time process.[3] Whilst batching may be more efficient in short runs, building up inventory is often a protection against inefficient/ineffective processes. This is considered a bane of Lean Operations, as batching tends to allow process problems to remain hidden. Figure 6.4 illustrates an idealised customer-driven or

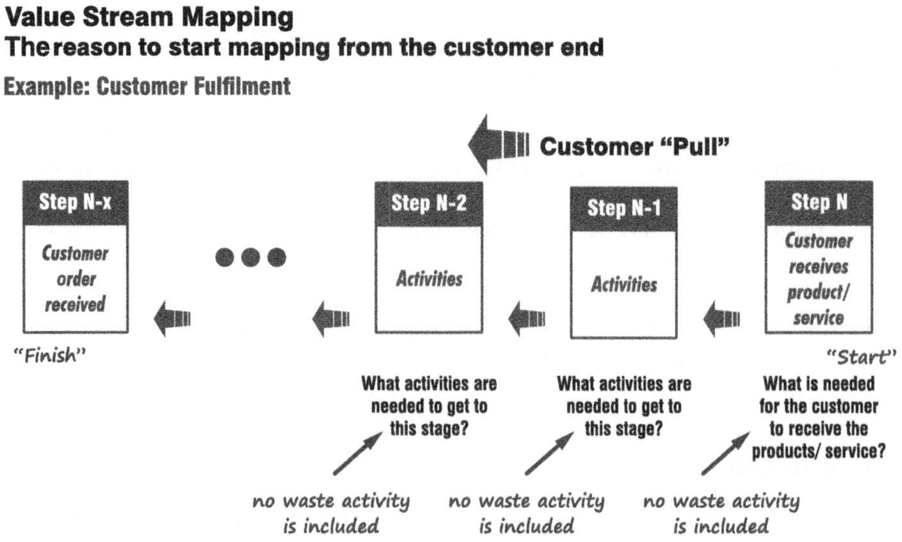

Value Stream Mapping
The reason to start mapping from the customer end

Example: Customer Fulfilment

Figure 6.4 Value Stream Mapping – Starting from the Customer End.

"Pull" situation where anything that does not add value to the customer is eliminated.

So when starting at the final dispatch to the end user, customer or the next downstream process, the question to ask is:

What needs to be done to get us to this stage?

The answer should only contain value-adding activities to allow the finished product/service to be delivered at the next step. In other words, we need to be driven by customer "Pull" (see Appendix 2 for more information). Once you have listed the value-adding activities, you can then go to the previous step (see Figure 6.4) and repeat the question until you get to the starting point – usually when the customer places and order.

By looking at the previous step, you can quickly see whether the necessary actions are being taken and whether these are both efficiently and effectively being carried out. You then log any that you reckon can be improved. Also, you can ask the team working there for their honest opinion, making sure they understand your intent is to make it easier for them to deliver a result and not to hammer them. With the value-adding activities listed, you can then explore what value-enabling activities will enhance the delivery. If either the value-adding or value-enabling process step does not appear efficient or effective, then this becomes the start of an improvement action.

Other information to collect is about the process parameters:

- What is needed to carry out this activity?
- What is the designed pace of the activity?
- What is the output quality?

By comparing the actual process data with the as-designed process parameters, you can quickly assess whether this area has any problems in asset Availability, process Performance or output Quality. These three parameters also allow you to calculate the Overall Effectiveness of the particular process step.[4]

We examined the Overall Effectiveness concept in Chapter 2, where it is used to explore Energy Productivity. Here the same tool is aimed at the working level of the operations.

Overall Effectiveness = Availability rate × Performance rate × Quality rate

The parameters you can measure are dependent on your process. Sometimes you will find that it is not the actions themselves that are causing waste, but changeovers to the next piece of work or handovers to the next workstation.

For example, we often measure cycle time per product/transaction as a part of assessing the performance of the process, but we should also look at the non-value-adding time between activities in the process (see Figure 4.4). If there is a delay that does not make sense, then dig a bit deeper, and as always, the questions to ask can include:

- What happened? This gives you an idea what is going on.
- How did this happen? This gives you an indication of the causes.
- What's the impact? This gives you a measure of the seriousness of the problem.

The Current State Value Stream Map is built up with detailed information about the way value is added to the process currently. You may find your Current State Value Stream not optimised, it may not be efficient or effective, but it is the baseline from which you can carry out improvements.

Sometimes it is also possible for you to collect too much data – stuff that you don't need. Nowadays, data can be relatively easy to collect with electronic sensors, as discussed in Chapter 5, and with spreadsheet software, you can analyse for all kinds of correlations; for causes as well as a myriad of interpolations and extrapolations until the details make your eyes pop and you lose sight of the overall process.

One way to avoid being overwhelmed with data is to assess the critical parameters. A Criticality Assessment is a frequently encountered event in Lean and Six Sigma.[5] It is similar in concept to the choke point shown in the Swim Lanes process maps in Figure 4.8 in Chapter 4. Essentially, you look at the aspects that are critical to deliver the results. They can be people, the tools and techniques, the raw materials or the communications. Whatever they are, as long as you use the measures consistently within your process, you can address the various parameters within the Current State Value Stream Map. Often, a Criticality Assessment is described as a Tree Diagram, as in Figures 4.5 and 6.5. This is a very simple but effective tool applicable to many process improvement analyses.

Figure 6.5 uses the Overall Effectiveness parameters as a starting point for a Criticality Assessment; this Tree Diagram deconstructs the parameters and describes the critical factors. Similarly, a Criticality Assessment for Energy Effectiveness can be carried out by looking at what will affect the use of energy in the activity.

After reviewing all the value-adding activities, you should then assess the value-enabling actions. Are they all effectively and efficiently carried out? For example:

- Legal compliance: Has it been done? Does it comply? Is the action recorded properly? Are the records stored properly?
- Health and safety: Has a risk assessment been carried out regularly/recently? Are the safety procedures in place? Are they being followed? Is the personal protection equipment being used properly? Are there safety

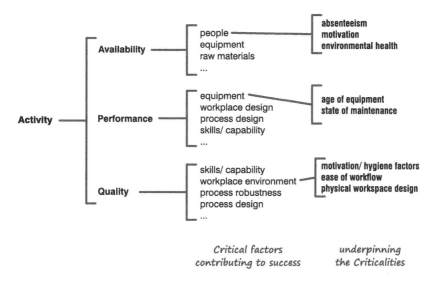

Figure 6.5 Criticality Tree – Example.

breaches? Are these recorded properly? Are the corrective actions taken every time the action is repeated?
• Quality assurance: Are the procedures up-to-date? Are they accurate? Is the staff capable of carrying out the assessment? Can we meet the quality specifications?
• Staff development: Do your teams have the right skills, knowledge and capabilities to carry out the necessary activities? Have they been trained in waste reduction?

Any actions that are considered value adding or value enabling but are actually not well carried out (deemed inadequate, inefficient or ineffective) are therefore part of the overall improvement action. You can therefore identify the value-adding and value-enabling activities as well as isolate those activities that are neither (i.e. waste).

Imagine you are designing a Future State from scratch by starting from the final step – you will generally only add both value-adding and value-enabling steps and activities as needed until you reach the natural starting point.

This brings us to "bureaucracy," often a significant part of many organisations. Can it be optimised? Well, to be truthful, I think it is technically possible to break down the bureaucratic activities into their elements and assess the overall effectiveness. However, we hit a big obstacle in this exercise – What is the value from the bureaucratic activities?[6] When does bureaucracy add or enable value?

Like a lot things, bureaucracy has a bad name. At its purest, it is probably value enabling, but poor publicity means it is often derided as a waste of time or pointless activity. Of course, if you ask a bureaucrat, the answer is likely to be "it is value adding!" But if it is a case of poor marketing (they're bureaucrats!) and poor explanation (arrogant bureaucrats!), then maybe the solution is to include a dose of marketing with any process improvement. Therefore, if we did manage to bring true value-adding or value-enabling elements to hitherto bureaucratic activities, then maybe it should no longer be called bureaucracy but probably just a part of an improved business process.

But wait a minute; bureaucracy is sometimes necessary (a necessary evil, perhaps?). In the UK National Health Service, I spoke with colleagues whose jobs seemed to consist entirely of bureaucracy – nagging people for information on process performance. When I asked them about it, I was told that gathering such information (which does not necessarily make a patient better, hence my definition of bureaucracy and what Toyota deems as waste) was critical because this is how the hospital gets paid by the healthcare system. So it is essentially a value-enabling activity without which the hospital's income will drop and patients will not be treated.

Therefore, we may encounter some form of value-enabling activities disguised as bureaucracy. Is it a process issue or is it a marketing issue? I reckon it is probably a marketing issue because the teams gathering this data should be able to better explain what their important roles are to their colleagues. (Instead of a virtuous circle, is this a circle of bureaucracy? The activities are deemed bureaucracy because the people doing it can't sell it better. They can't sell it better because they don't see the need to do so. They don't see the need to do so perhaps because they are bureaucrats and functionaries ...)

How do we spot such disguised value-enabling activities? One Lean approach we can adopt is the "red tagging" using sticky notes,[7] as shown in Figure 6.6 to highlight any action that does not make sense or cannot be explained easily by the people working in the process. The onus is therefore for the activity owner to explain and justify the activity. This can then be assessed by a Criticality Assessment.

A simple "red tag" for an incomprehensible activity that needs explaining by the activity owner

Figure 6.6 Red Tag.

Analysing the problem

Let's get something clarified now – problems usually result in waste in one form or another: time, effort, materials, motivation, money and so on. Since all these things will have some impact on effective use of resources (including energy), waste therefore affects the energy productivity of our organisation. By lowering the energy productivity, waste becomes the "Anti-Sustainability."

No matter what sustainability initiatives you are running, if you do not tackle waste, then your Energy Productivity KPI will not improve and your sustainability efforts will not realise their full potential. With this in mind, our focus on process problems is about both visible and hidden waste. There are a number of definitions of waste; Toyota, the inventor of Lean Operations, reckons there are three main types of waste and its 7 *Hidden Wastes*, as shown in Figure 6.7.

The visible waste is, well, visible: rubbish bins full of unnecessary printed outputs or photocopies; construction site skips with cables and lighting, bricks and timber; food waste from canteens; and so on. But what of the hidden waste? These are actually still visible, but we see them so often we no longer notice them.[8] My NoWaste® programme defines a set of 10 *specific common hidden waste*. This is shown alongside Toyota's 7 *Hidden Wastes* in Figure 6.7. The 10 are derived from the Toyota model but adapted for general business use.

The impact on energy productivity from these 10 common hidden wastes is quite significant – on Operational Energy but especially for Systems Energy. Table 6.3 illustrates how simple waste can impact repeatedly in an organisation.

Figure 6.7 Classifying Commonly Encountered Waste.

Table 6.3 The 10 Common Hidden Wastes

| | Impacts on | |
| | | |
Common Waste	Operational Energy Use	Systems Energy Use
Waiting	Energy use when equipment is left idling and not turned off	Energy is used even when no work is being done. Delays mean even more energy waste.
Rushing	Likely minor increase as rushing often overrides resource-efficient operations	Minimum impact as little change from steady state, unless operating in overtime
Too many changes	More work done and more energy used to deliver the outputs	Little impact, unless activities run late in overtime
Over transport	More energy used	More movement may mean more motion sensitive lights turning on, also may require more HVAC★/lighting in passageways for health and safety reasons
Over order	Little added impact other than transaction processing	More energy used to maintain and store larger inventory
Not working to plan	Messing up timetable is likely to lead to rework/corrections and so more energy used	Can delay overall timetable for activity and so increases energy use
Errors and defects	Correcting mistakes and rework can mean double or more time energy use to deliver the same outcome	Systems energy is wasted and unproductive due to the errors/defects
Lost ideas	Lost opportunity for improvement	Lost opportunity for improvement
Uneven effort	Variation in quality may require rework to correct	Inefficient use of Systems Energy due to the likelihood of rework
Pointless effort	Total waste of energy	Total waste of energy

★ HVAC – acronym for Heating, Ventilation and Air Conditioning.

E-mails and Internet searches – how to create waste without thinking

We have been hectored to death about (not) printing emails, but things may be worse than we think. France 24, a TV station, reckons[9] that each Internet search has an energy or carbon cost of 5–7g of CO_2, and each email has a carbon cost of 20g of CO_2 – and a "cc" email costs 6g of CO_2 – so do not hit *reply all* unless it is really necessary! What does all this mean? France 24 tells us that sending an email with a cc email together (26g CO_2) is equivalent to keeping a light bulb going for an hour, and sending 30 emails each day for a year is equivalent to the CO_2 emissions of a 1000 km car ride.[10] The moral of the story, it was pointed out, is to think about all the unread (and unwanted) emails in your inbox. On 14 November 2016, the UK's National Health Service sent itself about 500 million emails in 75 minutes through a messed up test message to about 850,000 recipients. About 80 people then hit "reply all" to demand their removal from the send list and you can guess the rest – melt down.[11] The energy implications of this mess were not debated, while the NHS blamed its contractor. But based on the France 24 sums, it would appear the energy cost of the NHS snafu was roughly 1000 tonnes of CO_2 emissions, or the same as driving to Paris from London about 10,000 times or so. (And after Brexit, this alone will probably keep the Customs and Excise people employed for a while.)

Workplace improvements

Studying the Value Stream and Process Maps can help us identify some of the 10 Common Hidden Wastes, but it is probably more effective if you also conduct a walk through as well. On this waste-spotting walk through, I would advise you to focus initially on the 10 Common Hidden Wastes as well as workplace organisation or 5S[12] (see Figure 6.8 for more details). 5S stands for Sort/Set/Shine/Standardise/Sustain.[13] This is a series of activities performed in this particular order to make the workplace more effective, less wasteful and safer. The Red Tag approach works well in a 5S walk through since you can use the red tags as ready reckoners of items to follow up.

A 5S walk through is often used in workplace improvements, discussed earlier and shown in Figure 6.2, and it will help identify the reasons for a messy workplace as well as poorly managed storage areas. The first three 5S actions: Sort, Set and Shine are used to carry out an initial clear out and tidying up and contribute to a more energy efficient workplace by eliminating clutter, unnecessary and unwanted items and the resources needed to

Figure 6.8 5S Benefits and Outcomes.

manage them. These are quite straightforward to implement and described later in Tables 6.4 to 6.6.

The Standardise element is a more intense activity, as it examines whether standardised working practices[14] are part of the working methodology. A 5S survey can identify non-standard working practices that can lead to variations in output quality. It is also a reflection of the Uneven Effort hidden waste.

Standardised practice is a way of ensuring optimal energy use, provided that your practice is also optimal, of course. It should also be the safer way of working too, because people are not using unofficial or untested methods where potential risks were not identified and dealt with, also a disadvantage of workarounds. So, if you spot non-standardised work, you should consider it an opportunity to find out what happened, how it happened and why it happened. This is described in Figure 6.9.

The Sustain action in 5S comprises an entirely different set of activities. Sort/Set/Shine, the first three Ss, are about activities that can keep a workplace clear, tidy and safe. Standardise, the fourth S, is about designing an effective process or methodology and then making sure that the relevant people are trained to use it. The final S, however, is about ensuring that good practice is maintained and there is no slipping back. It is about behaviour change and brings in other elements such as training, development, communications, recognition and rewards.

Carrying out a 5S improvement action

Most 5S observations do not need profound analysis – a mess is a mess. Therefore, in many cases, a 5S walk through can lead directly into a 5S workplace improvement action.

Red tagging and photographs will create a record of the Current State and what needs to be done where. While these are both useful, probably the most

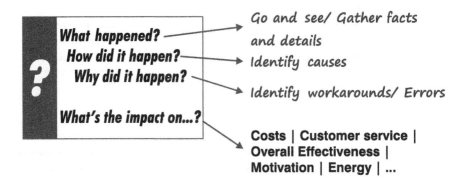

Figure 6.9 Non-Standard Working Practices.

important technique is a temporary suspension of judgement. When something is not right, just mention it, log it, tag it or photograph it. There is not a lot to gain by labouring the point to the team involved. People either notice the mess and do nothing for whatever reason or they got the Hidden Waste syndrome and just don't notice it. Going ballistic about a mess just misses the point (unless there is a serious health and safety infringement); what is more important is why nothing was done – are people that busy or is it that they just don't care? Both are causes for concern and should be treated as problems to be resolved rather than the visible mess on the surface. In these instances think of an iceberg as shown in Figure 6.10 – what are the underlying problems that lead to this situation?

Tables 6.4–6.6 outline the first three 5S elements and their general impacts generally through two sets of examples – the physical workplace and the computer desktop/shared drive workplace (the Virtual Workplace).

Figure 6.10 Iceberg.

Table 6.4 **5S – Sort** Activities

Physical Workplace	Virtual Workplace (computer/IT)
Sorting to make sure all raw materials are used in proper sequence (first in – first use)	Make sure information and data are up to date
Arrange equipment so that cables, hoses etc. are not causing hazards	Make sure security software/patches are up-to-date
Eliminate clutter and unwanted items	Make sure data protection requirements are complied with
Dispose of unused and non-essential items	Make sure backups are up-to-date and stored in the proper location

Table 6.5 **5S – Set** Activities

Physical Workplace	Virtual Workplace (computer/IT)
Check all labels and replace if necessary	Set up a filing system that eases information retrieval
Simplify access to regularly used items	Use a file naming system that helps people find information easily
Maintain and update a log of items stored in each area	Label versions clearly
Reduce unnecessary duplicate storage	When sharing files, make sure the correct protocols are followed
Use a standard layout system for storage	Use shared drives sensibly
Make sure everything is in the right place regularly by introducing Shadow Boards[15] and other visual management tools	Label shared folders and local folders in a logical and sensible way: easy to understand, simple to find and practical to use

Table 6.6 **5S – Shine** Activities

Physical Workplace	Virtual Workplace (computer/IT)
Cleaning and clearing the work area regularly	Use the correct software to clean and tidy up the virtual workplace regularly
Tidy the work area to make it easier to check for problems and hazards, and more pleasant for everyone working there	Tidy the desktop and shared drive as trying to find something in an anarchic share drive is a serious time waster

5S – Standardise activities for both physical and virtual workplaces

- Standardise work procedures to minimise variations (standard software, algorithms, procedures and templates for computers/share drives)
- Review progress in Sort, Set and Shine
- Develop a standard operating procedure
- Allocate responsibility for all activities
- Establish a standard approach that is easy, simple and practical, and get everyone to follow

5S – Sustain activities for both physical and virtual workplaces

- Simplify activities, procedures and processes to make it easier to sustain the improvement – Design/Redesign activities, procedures and processes to be easy to carry out
- Make sure that the designed/redesigned activities, procedures and processes are practical to the people doing the work
- Carry out and encourage continuous improvements
- Report success and progress – communicate to the teams involved

- Review procedures regularly and update if necessary
- Encourage individuals to take responsibility for success

An easy way to start a 5S action is to select an area for the activity, take "before photos" of the Current State, carry out the improvement, take "after photos" and then move on to the next 5S action. The before/after photos are also very useful in boosting team morale as well as demonstrating progress.

5S and reuse

One other very useful feature of 5S is that it forms a very effective protocol for the Reuse activity in the Waste Hierarchy. Efficient and effective Reuse actions rely on making it easy for people to store and find useful items (Table 6.7). Oh, and you should also carry out a 5S analysis on the Reuse areas too.

Table 6.7 5S for Reuse

	Classical 5S	*5S for Reuse*
Sort	Sort out items that are going to be used, and get rid of the unwanted and unnecessary	i Sort out items that are going to be used ii Sort the remaining items for reuse or recycle/disposal
Set	Store things effectively such that they can be readily retrieved and used	i Provide a suitable storage area for reuse, and protect the items from damage ii Have a simple system to record item movements
Shine	A clean and tidy workplace is a safer, more pleasant and more effective workplace	A clean and tidy storage area for reuse means you can easily find it again, and in an undamaged form ready for use
Standardise	Working to standardised methods means a consistency of quality and safety	Sticking to the standardised methods for handling reuse means that items are not thrown away by mistake A consistent reuse policy means everyone can participate easily Allow people to find things to reuse easily
Sustain	Sustain the 5S efforts by continuous improvement, rewards and training	Sustain 5S for Reuse by sharing its success with everyone Train everyone to take part in reuse Continuously improve the way we manage Reuse

The 5S walk-through action sometimes highlights issues that cannot be easily resolved by on-the-spot improvements, as they may be an indication of deeper issues. For example, a messy workplace can indicate several things: people are slobs, people are too busy to tidy up, people don't care or people just accept it as part of the company culture. While some of these can be fixed temporarily with a clean and clear up, they may also represent underlying issues that need to be dealt with through a more thorough analysis. This is where the DMAIC (Define, Measure, Analyse, Improve and Control) problem analysis comes in.

DMAIC - the standard Six Sigma problem-solving technique

DMAIC is a packaging of more or less what we discussed in both this chapter so far and Chapter 4. It is an integrated framework for problem spotting and improvement, as shown in Figure 6.11.

The first step, **Define**, is not just about finding out what the problem is, but making sure the information is shared with and agreed between the relevant people. Defining a problem is often more difficult than first thought – people have different interpretations of what they perceive as the problem, as it is likely to affect them differently.

There are several aims in the defining action. You want everyone to be on the same page, so there needs to be an agreed version of what happened (or is happening). In order for everyone to agree on what the problem is and also to be able to explain the problem, there needs to be a simple, clear and precise definition in place such that every person involved can describe it in a consistent way. While you may think this is a bit pedantic and even bossy, it is necessary to make sure everyone is on the same page (i.e. dealing with the same problem). It is necessary because we all have colleagues who like to waffle; for them it is often "Why use 1 sentence when you can use 3 paragraphs plus appendices and small print?"

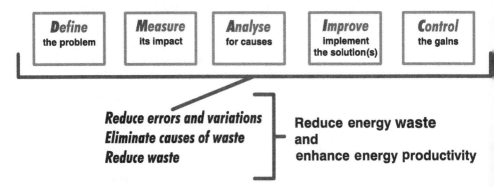

Figure 6.11 DMAIC – Six Sigma Problem Solving.

For a complex problem at work, this isn't always as easy as it appears. The surface problem noticed by team members may hide something more complex underneath, just like the metaphor of an iceberg. So it is likely that the team will need to work together to come up with an agreed definition.

Measure is about getting details of the problem, information that can help you reach a decision on the way forward. There are many ways of getting that information: you can ask someone, go and see or check the recorded data. What you should not do is to estimate (or guess!) without up-to-date information. So it is back to *gemba*: Go and See – Go to where it is happening. Although I mentioned the importance of this in the description on Overall Effectiveness earlier in this book, this is such an important issue that I am reiterating it, because no matter how familiar we are with the situation, something new may be happening that is beyond our envelope of experience. Therefore it is important to go and have a look or have someone report the facts (and making sure it is the facts and not their interpretation). The points I made in Chapter 5 about managing data is entirely applicable to the measure action.

What about data from enterprise resource planning software? These are accurate in reporting the performance when linked to plant and equipment and integrated with databases. However, they do not necessarily reflect the human element within a business process, so whilst the information can highlight potential issues in a process, it is still necessary to get confirmation by inspection or from direct reporting.

There are several reasons for the emphasis on measuring the impact: one is to allow us to assess the level of the impact and therefore prioritise available resources to deal with it. Another is to allow us to assess the energy impacts. Sometimes a small process hiccup may have a much larger energy impact – for example, a UK blood testing lab moved their frozen blood samples from one freezer to another, a legacy of having only a small fast freezer many years ago. This is where electronic trend data may not tell you, as it is about habits and behaviour, whereas a site visit is likely to lead to asking "Why?"

There are many ways to prioritise problems; you can use cost impacts, time impacts or quality impacts. As universal parameters are common to many problems, you can compare them side-by-side. The Pareto Rule is a simple technique to assess relative impacts – you simply rearrange the problems in order of their impacts. The Pareto principle shows that most of the impacts are often from a few problems.[16] This approach is explored further in Chapter 8.

Analyse the Causes and Criticality, or the fun and boring bit, of DMAIC – solving problems! Fun because it is solving problems; you are making progress and maybe rolling back the frontiers of knowledge. Boring because I suggest you do it methodically, otherwise you are likely to be solving the same problem again in the future if you are not methodical in eliminating the Root Cause.[17] This is analogous to Six Sigma thinking about solving a problem once and for all. Unfortunately, being methodical is not necessarily fun for everyone but then again, neither is coming back and tackling it again and again.

DMAIC can be used as a tool framework, as shown in Figure 6.12. Various tools and techniques can be slotted into the DMAIC analysis at various stages.

Finding the most likely cause

The Cause–Effect or Fishbone analysis[18] is ideal as a team-based analysis tool where you want the team to gain consensus about the most likely cause to a problem. It is based on observations, the team of people actively involved with the process and the problem. It has a number of stages and a few unusual activities as shown below, including a step "0."[19] The common name, "fishbone," comes from the resemblance to a fish skeleton.

0   **Preparations** – Unlike many analyses, the Cause–Effect analysis has a lot of value-enabling activities that make the analysis go easier but not listed as a formal step (hence step 0!). These include finding suitable space to carry out the analysis: sticky notes, pens, stickers, flipchart sheets, white boards, someone taking photos of the analysis (as a record) and someone coordinating the analysis process.

1   **Identify problem** – This is a fairly standard action in this type of analysis, but in the case of problem solving, it pays to be as precise as possible in order to avoid being sidetracked into broader issues.

Choose likely cause categories – these form the "spines" of the fishbone. Often in the Fishbone analysis, you see six spines although there is no reason why there should not be more or less or even an odd number of spines (although the fish bone will then look lopsided). If the categories do not come to mind easily, there is a set of "common causes" that cover a very broad range of possible but distinct cause categories. Figure 6.13 shows the often-used set of Common Causes.

Make sure there is agreement about the Common Causes within the team. It is better to have the arguments early to clarify the issues rather than not being on the same page later.

A digression about arguments or differing opinions in this analysis: the whole point is to get the team to agree on a most likely cause, and thence it is likely there will be discussions and disagreements. An effective way to deal with these differences in opinions is to ask the proposing individual to explain his/her point and convince the other team members of the viability of the argument. This is where data, capability, knowledge and experience all play a role in creating a sense of conviction. While data can usually carry the day, it is improved by experience and knowledge. Relying on opinion alone is not recommended; data (or numbers) is always necessary to support any qualitative or emotional argument.

What about intuition then? Gut feel is an important part of many decision-making processes, and we should value this. Nonetheless, intuition

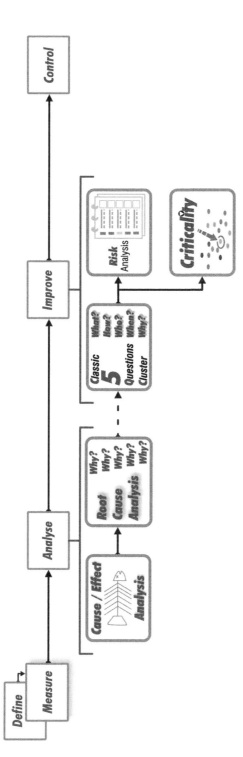

Figure 6.12 Using DMAIC as an Analysis Framework.

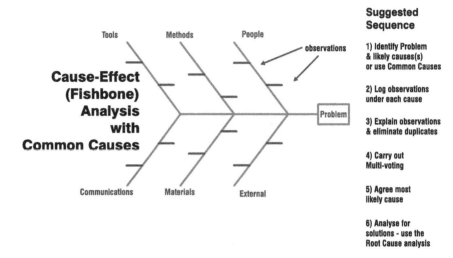

Figure 6.13 Cause-Effect Analysis.

needs to be backed with a bit of science and data even if we accept the wisdom of very knowledgeable, capable and experienced colleagues.

Once the likely causes have been agreed on, it is easier to draw the fishbone onto a (large) wall board or onto several sheets of flipchart paper. The large size is really to make the subsequent activities easier to manage.

2 **List observations** – There are many ways to do this; I usually get my colleagues to write the observations on sticky notes and stick them onto the relevant cause category spine. You may wish to limit both the time allowed and number of sticky notes so as to encourage people to think through their observations but not get bogged down.

Observations can be both qualitative (feelings – "I don't feel comfortable using the new power tools") and quantitative (numbers – "the material is 2 months past its use by date").

Another point to bear in mind is to engage the quieter members of the team when using this analysis – you don't want the loud colleagues to dominate the discussions. Give the quieter colleagues both time and perhaps physical space to say their bit, and encourage them to defend their points if required.

Don't forget what is behind all the observations: waste and wasted energy. Energy is not represented in this analysis – it is not a cause, but it is behind everything at work, so I suggest you consider observations that can have an impact on energy use too. For example:

- "Our people are not skilled, their mistakes waste energy" (cause categories: people, methods, tools or communications)
- "Our building is not well insulated, we are leaking heat" (cause category: external – because it is not process-related)

3   **Clarify observations and eliminate duplicates** – The coordinator then goes through the mass of sticky notes and seeks clarification from the owner if there is confusion. This is when the individual defends the particular sticky note observation. Do not get involved in extensive debate on every point; otherwise, you and your team may be there all night.

Sometimes it is possible that two or more colleagues are saying the same thing but saying it differently on their sticky notes. This is when the coordinator needs to tease out the details of the observations and eliminate duplicates to simplify the fishbone. Figure 6.14 shows teams carrying out the Cause-Effect analysis at one of my workshops.

4   **Multi-voting** – This is the fun part of the Cause-Effect analysis. Every member of the team is given a fixed number of "votes" to place on what they individually consider the most likely observation (i.e. the cause of the problem).

There are different views on how many votes to allocate: some suggest a few less than the number of observations; others suggest a random number like 20 (not too few, not too many). My own inclination is the "20" since I usually have the vote indicators (in reality, stickers) prepared before the exercise. This leads us to the actual votes themselves.

In reality, this is where the prepared "stickers" come in; a vote in this case is indicated by where the sticker goes on the fishbone framework – classier colleagues (or those with bigger budgets) use sheets of sticky dots. I use stacks of sticky notes cut (or torn) to strips. Everyone is given their votes and asked to allocate as many of their votes to what they consider the most likely cause; then to the next most likely cause and so on until they run out of votes. An individual can therefore put all the votes onto a single likely cause or none.

5   The votes are counted and the most popular vote becomes the **Most Likely Cause**.

Eliminating duplicates   **Multi-voting**

Figure 6.14 Cause-Effect Analysis – Example (photos).

6   **Analyse the Most Likely Cause** of the problem. I recommend that the Fishbone analysis stops at this point and a Root Cause analysis be carried out. This is to make sure we do not jump to conclusions immediately on achieving the most likely cause and instead adopt a more methodical and thorough approach. The Root Cause analysis is described in the next section.

Reality check – now that the most likely cause has been agreed on, it is important to check that it is not a theoretical cause but actually a real cause. This check is important because of a phenomenon called Group Think – where a cohesive, self-confident group decides to follow its own judgements and ignore conventional thinking or outside concepts and avoid reviewing alternative courses of action. Group Think is often characterised by the following traits:[20]

- Play down the team's own weaknesses (team decisions are always correct)
- Beliefs that the team's aims and means are superior
- Sweeping under the carpet any new information that does not correspond with the team's beliefs
- Stereotyping of new information into established themes without deeper consideration
- Members of the team suppress doubts to maintain cohesiveness
- Guarding bad news from reaching others in the team

The Reality Check is important since the team will be going forward on their shared agreement of the most likely cause.

Doing a Cause-Effect analysis without a team (i.e. by yourself)

I mentioned earlier that the Cause-Effect or Fishbone analysis is great as a team-based analysis, but it is also effective when you are on your own. It is true that you will not have everyone's ideas; nonetheless, the analysis provides a framework for a methodical analysis. This is extremely valuable since you have virtually all the components of Group Think in yourself. By forcing yourself to look at the problem through listing observations across the various likely causes, you make sure you are not fixated by a particular opinion and instead use data to support your decision making.

Getting to the Root Cause

As I mentioned earlier, the momentum from a Fishbone analysis is to go straight from the most likely cause to develop one or more possible solutions, however, there are good reasons for going through the Root Cause analysis (other than being pedantic). The Root Cause analysis helps us to see any intermediate causes that may offer partial solutions.

Intermediate Causes? What are they?

The Root Cause analysis helps us find the intermediate causes before you get to the final or Root Cause. These intermediate causes offer partial solutions, which, while not desirable in an ideal world, are often the only options in real-world situations.

The Root Cause analysis, shown in Figure 6.15, is very simple and straightforward: just ask "why?" and start the answer with "because…" The "because…" then becomes the next "why?" and so on, cascading it to the fifth "why?"[21]

By answering the "why?" a reason is given through the "because." This is a possible cause of the problem, and by addressing the "because," the problem is at that stage of the questioning. However, this is a partial solution and may not prevent the problem from re-appearing, as we have not reached the Root Cause. When we get to the Root Cause, then a solution will mean the problem will not occur thereafter.

The following example actually happened in a London office of a housing association (Table 6.8).

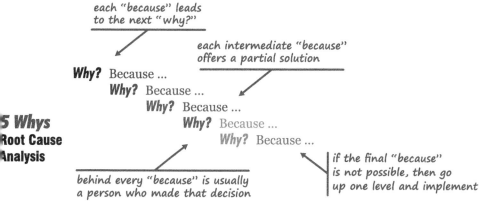

Figure 6.15 Root Cause Analysis.

Table 6.8 Root Cause Analysis Example – "The Work in the Office Came to a Halt One Morning"

Why	Because	Possible Solution
Why did the work come to a halt?	Because we couldn't print any documents.	Go to a high street printer and get it done.
Why couldn't we print anything?	Because we ran out of paper completely.	Go buy two boxes of paper.
Why did we run out of paper?	Because nobody knew we were running low.	Order 20 boxes every week.
Why didn't anyone know?	Because we have seven paper storage cabinets in the office and nobody checks all of them.	Get someone to check the paper stock level every evening.
Why do we have seven cabinets???	Because nobody was responsible for organising office supplies.	Assign someone to be responsible NOW!!!

Despite the simplicity of the Root Cause Analysis, the example above shows that there are a few elements to pay particular attention to when you are carrying out a Root Cause analysis.

1   Intermediate Solutions: Every "because" leads to an intermediate solution. Each of these can get you out of a hole now, but the problem may come back because the solution is not at the Root Cause level.

2   Behind a "because…" there is often a person who made the original decision. I call this person a "Critical Contact;" critical because s/he is essential to your improvement going smoothly since s/he has a stake in the situation, critical also because you may be overturning his/her previous decision. You can image that this person may be somewhat concerned about this (to say the least).

   Since these people are often local champions or leaders of some sort, they can be crucial in influencing behaviour change (and that's often what an improvement ends up in practice), so you should think about how to get them on side. But how do you entice someone whose decision you are about to overturn? Perhaps you can flatter them or influence these people. Perhaps you can say "the world has changed" (this is always true) and therefore their formerly wonderful decision is less effective now (this is also a fact). What is needed is a new way forward to help the team and therefore would s/he help you?

   If the Critical Contact is a prima donna (see Figure 4.16), you can try to manipulate them, either by saying this is too minor to bother them (and therefore sideline them) with, or flatter them by attributing the solution to a comment of his/hers a while back. This often works since most people cannot remember incidental comments made a few months ago. Note that this ploy is used for its expediency only, and since it made them feel good and/or important, they are likely to agree and let you get on with it, which was your original plan.

   As long as you load up with the facts and save his/her face with some flattering, you should be able to get the Critical Contacts on board.

3   The Unachievable Final "because" happens because you don't have the budget, the talent, the resources or the time to make it happen. So just go up one level of "because" and implement the intermediate solution. This is akin to sticking on a bandage, but if it gets you through to the next budgeting period or whatever, it will have to do. Just remember to carry out the implementation when the situation allows – as long as it is still relevant.

4   There may be more than one Root Cause. The example from Table 6.8 shows that there may be other pathways towards the Root Cause. This brings us back to the Criticality Assessment.

   We may need to explore a Criticality Tree of the most likely cause to see whether there are several streams each offering specific solutions. In the London housing association example in Table 6.7, we have several criticalities as shown below:

Criticality 1: the teams that use paper – timetables, pattern of usage, need for paper etc.
Criticality 2: general office management – any procedures for purchasing, information on stock levels etc.
Criticality 3: people who run the "office store" – capabilities, resources etc.
    In this case, there may be three Root Causes, and there will be a need to coordinate the three improvement actions.

5   How the improvement action will impact energy use is a point that you also need to take into account. If it is more energy efficient or marginally more efficient, then the action should go ahead. While it is unlikely that an improvement action will result in greater energy waste, it is possible that the solution may consume more energy (for example, to deliver a higher quality output). Before any decisions can be made, you need to analyse the data and correlate them to the needs and capabilities of the business. Ultimately, it is a business decision, and if a higher quality output can improve sales, you can adopt it and then use continuous improvement to become more efficient.

The Solution
    The solution(s) arising from these analyses is often a technically correct solution, for example:

*   reduce quality defects
*   cut down waiting times
*   measure twice, cut once…

These are all very sound suggestions, and what's more, they are the correct solution; except they may not be the right one.

    The right solution is one that survives its encounter with the people at work. Just imagine you have gone through an extensive, comprehensive and methodical analysis and you are about to present your improvement solution to possibly indifferent or irascible colleagues. This and other associated delights will be explored further in Chapter 7.

    Now we have covered the first three elements of DMAIC: Define, Measure and Analyse. These three are the planning and analysing part of DMAIC. In the next chapter we tackle action part of DMAIC: Improve and Control, and be warned, they are the hard ones!

Notes

1   True only if you are moving a few bits of plant, equipment or furniture around. If extensive building work is involved, it may no longer be the cheapest or quickest option.

2 Legislative compliance is also required but not necessarily the fundamental reason you have a business process; it may, however, be an "enabling value" reason.

3 Cautionary note: A super efficient just-in-time system may fall over if external events, such as earthquakes, mess up your logistics or supply chain and you have no stocks. See Appendix 2 for a short description of what happened to Toyota's super efficient system when disaster struck.

4 This is also the same procedure to measure the Overall Effectiveness of the process. See Appendix 2.

5 This is not in Appendix 2 because it is just fancy jargon for what is critical. It is also more or less the same as a Cascading Tree Diagram (see Figure 4.11), but sounds more impressive.

6 In some countries, GDP devoted to the public sector goes up year to year; is this always adding value? See *The Politics of Bureaucracy*, B. G. Peters, 6th Edition, Routledge, 2010.

7 Not necessarily red, but you get the point.

8 The Hidden Wastes are a major element in Lean Operations.

9 Down to Earth: The Hidden Pollution of the Internet, France 24, 3 March 2017.

10 Their numbers, not mine. But since it is on both the French and English version of France 24's website and also on TV and YouTube, it must be true.

11 Source: the Register website, 31 January 2017.

12 Another Toyota technique where the S-words are adopted from S-sounding Japanese words.

13 Since it is a Western adoption of a series of activities, you may have heard of it being called 5Cs, CAN DO and ANCOD – see Appendix 2 for more details.

14 This is another Lean principle to ensure consistency in flow, output quality, work pace as well as to reduce variations.

15 A Shadow Board is a physical board where the tool silhouettes are painted to show where the individual tool should reside; a missing tool is easily noticed on a Shadow Board. This is part of the Lean Visual Management approach. See Appendix 2 for more detail.

16 Sometimes known as the 80:20 rule – where 80 per cent of the impacts are caused by 20 per cent of the problems. See Appendix 2.

17 See Root Cause analysis in Appendix 2 for more information.

18 Sometimes also known as Ishikawa diagrams after Kaoru Ishikawa, who invented them. (Professor Ishikawa also invented quality circles and other quality tools.) See Appendix 2 for more details.

19 For some reason the preparations step is not often treated as part of the analysis. I added it because if you forget these things, your analysis may go less well.

20 The Group Think details came from my colleague Anastasia Marinopoulou of the Progress Through Consultancy.

21 Why five? Well, Toyota (yes, it is another of their techniques) reckons if you go beyond 5 cycles, then your original question is not sufficiently focussed.

7   The hard part

Implementing solutions and
controlling the *gains*

This chapter deals with the last two elements of DMAIC (Define, Measure, Analyse, Improve and Control): Improve and Control.

Improve

In the previous chapters, we explored the ways things can go wrong at work, which results in waste and reduced Energy Productivity. We then explored ways to tackle these problems and came up with solutions, which strictly should be called technical solutions. These are based on the work situation and are technically correct, as they tend to be tidy, neat and logical, but probably not workable in the real world.[1] The reasons for this are essentially three-fold: The real world is not always tidy, neat or logical; it is often chaotic, with messy lines of communications and often driven by emotions. In other words, our technical solution meets people like our colleagues at work, and that's when the best-laid plan can start to go awry. Figure 7.1 offers a glimpse of how far a technical solution can be from a real-world solution.

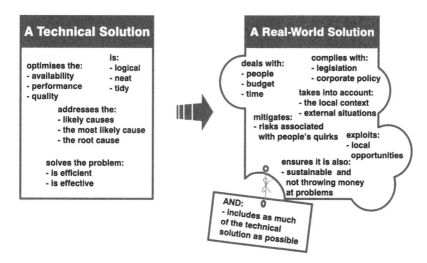

Figure 7.1 Technical vs. Real–World Solutions.

This is often the reason why a lot of change and innovation programmes fail: Real-world solutions need to take into account the local working environment and make adjustments accordingly.[2] Nonetheless, it is not practical for you to go around devising specific solutions for each individual area. However, it is possible to extend the *gemba* concept in terms of developing solutions. Who would usually know the local context best? I would suggest the team working there and perhaps their upstream and downstream colleagues. Therefore, it may be more effective for you to delegate the responsibility (and some of the accountability) for refining the solution to the local teams with experts being a support resource. A schematic description is shown in Figure 7.2.

A leader needs to engage the local team so that they can come up with ways forward that are applicable to the local context. However, you may still need to offer some guidance and coaching when it comes to planning the project. My advice is to make sure that whatever the team develops, it is "easy–simple–practical" – as outlined in Chapter 3 earlier when I was discussing how to deploy technology, but shown below for a more general case (Figure 7.3).

If you are an expert, then you will also need to follow these principles. This is especially so because you are an expert! Experts are supposed to understand the principles of their expertise area so well that they can explain it easily, simply and practically in the context of their audience. Expertise does mean you can show off a bit, but not using jargon and terms that confuse your audience. Often talking in jargon can mean the speaker does not really understand her/his topic that well. Having said that, perhaps an expert in rocket science or brain surgery needs to use rocket science or brain surgery jargon, but luckily for us, Everyday Sustainability and Energy Productivity are not elements of rocket science or brain surgery.

Easy brings at least two benefits: people won't get discouraged (think of how many unsolved Rubik's Cubes are sitting around in cupboards after people gave up on it); and more importantly, they won't make mistakes and waste their time, effort and energy. If you want your Energy Productivity to improve, then make it easy for people to deliver the improvement.

Simple is really saying don't make it complicated. Complicated things take time to learn, to sort out and to do. With most people being busy, it is also going to increase the likelihood of the activity being sidelined or abandoned. What is simplification then? It is about thinking through the required activities and designing them to minimise unnecessarily complex procedures or very long strings of activities without a break. Complex procedures are more prone to errors, and also people can get put off trying to understand a long list of instructions. By the way, simple also means a simple way or method to start an improvement project.

Unlike pre-literate society of yore, where people had to rely on their memory to remember anything (and everything), we are at an age of sound bites and 140–160 character messages. Let's be honest, since many of us can hardly remember the third item on the list of today's specials in a restaurant,[3]

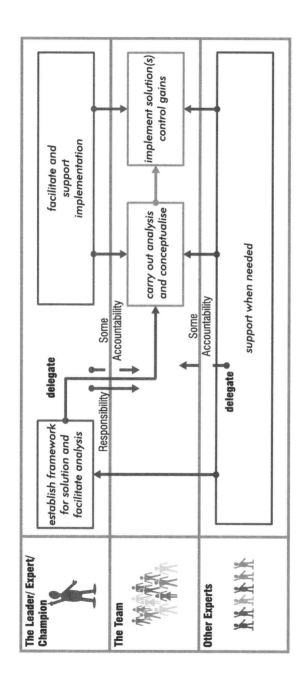

Figure 7.2 Solving Problems within the Local Context (Swim Lane View).

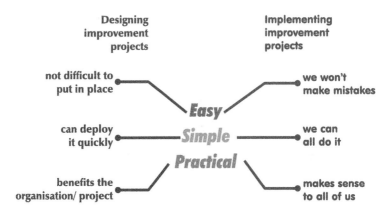

Figure 7.3 Easy – Simple – Practical.

complicated instructions are something many of us don't want or need. Of course, being responsible people, we won't just ignore complex instructions altogether but instead we may well put them aside to deal with when we have more time or we will skim them quickly and perhaps miss some important points. However, with the best of intentions, the chances of returning to understanding the complex task are likely to be slim – we know our working schedules. And we also know that when we eventually get around to it, it will still be as complicated as before.

The other benefit about simple is that everyone can take part, and being simple can mean quicker results too. These factors are important in process improvements but even more important when it comes to sustainability.

Practical is a different matter; this is where being in context really comes in. If the improvement project makes no sense to us, then why are we bothering? If we are told to "shut up and do it," then the project is likely to become the lowest common denominator, and we will do the minimum to get by. After all, why make a big effort when the activity has no meaning for us?

Therefore, even when it is simple and easy but we do not see it as practical or right for our context, we will likely feel that the decision makers are disconnected with us and have no idea what we are doing every day. This breaks down respect and trust and can lead to antagonism and conflict.

To encourage people to take part, it has to make sense. And more particularly, it needs to make sense in the right context or rather, our particular context. This requires taking the time and effort to understand your target audiences, their motives and drivers.

Remember, making it easy, simple and practical does not mean we are dumbing down or insulting people's intelligence, but we are eliminating poorly structured procedures or unclear instructions. There is no need to show off our knowledge of jargon and arcane management or sustainability knowledge; we want people to take part and we need to make sure when they start "doing," it will be easy to implement. It is also about thinking through the required activities and designing them to minimise the risk of errors and mistakes. In quality jargon, it is about ways to minimise variations.

Now that we have established a framework for the solution, we turn to the solution itself – what does it need to deliver?

Defining and assessing the needs

A clear definition of what needs to be done starts the process of planning and designing an improvement project. The needs, whether arising from a noticed problem or from a strategic objective, have to be defined. This can be done through a simple statement of intent about the improvement. This then takes into account the easy/simple/practical aspects and ideally should be in the form of a simple short sentence. If you cannot define it in a clear way, it is likely to confuse other people. For example:

1 "We aim to reduce energy waste on the fourth floor;" or
2 "We aim to cut waste to landfill"

The headline definitions are nothing special and do not include the attributes of the target or what achieving this target in real life means.

However, by defining the attributes of the target, we outline the "needs." This is a more detailed description of what needs to be done and generally best described with some numbers, for example:

1 "Our target is to raise the department's Energy Productivity by 10 per cent over six months"
2 "We aim to cut waste to landfill by 40 per cent in six months starting from June"

These two statements make it easier for people to understand, as the target now has substance. In many ways, the numbers clarify matters but may seem more nerdy if you are planning for a high-energy marketing message. In these instances, perhaps have the simple statement as a headline and have the numbers as a subtitle. Don't forget, having numbers for targets also means that you can measure the achievements of the project in a more meaningful way too.

Defining the needs should not be a difficult affair; you may be given a set of outcomes or targets to achieve – these are the needs. Or if you have been given a strategy to fulfil, you can readily look for actions that will lead to its realisation – whether as strategic aims, policies or targets. You may also wish to segment these into easily identifiable elements by using a business framework such as the Balanced Scorecard, as shown in Figure 7.4.

Now that you have defined the needs as the attributes of success, a simple What/How analysis will develop a set of possible activities for your improvement project. Then, bearing in mind the easy/simple/practical requirements, you can start to explore the options you have to deliver the results.

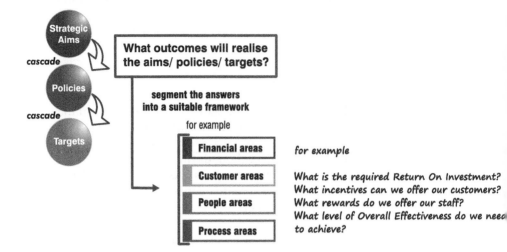

Figure 7.4 Creating a List of Needs.

I suggest calling the ideas you reckon will deliver the needs as "options" rather than "solutions." This is because they are options at this point and not fully worked out solutions yet. You may think I am being pedantic over the choice of words, but there is a reason for this. By calling these ideas options, there is less emotional stake involved, and also it does not have the finality of the word "solution." Therefore, if you have to reject an idea offered by a colleague, it is easier for everyone to move on from an "option" than a "solution."[4]

An easy way to manage a list of needs and a list of options is by using a matrix diagram outlining the effectiveness or impact of each option against the needs. This is shown in Figure 7.5 as three examples of a Relationship or Impact Matrix.[5]

The first example is a blank template with a list of the Needs and a list of the options in a matrix format.

The second example shows which options can contribute to delivering the needs. In the example, Option A can meet Needs 2 and 3, respectively, Option B can address Needs 1, 2 and 4 and so on.

The third example provides more detail to show how effective each option is. I suggest using a simple 1–5 scale to describe the effectiveness of each option where 1 represents low effectiveness and 5 represents high effectiveness. Note, however, this is a subjective estimate based on the experience and knowledge of you and your colleagues.

In the third example, we can see that

Option 1 deals with Need 2 somewhat and Need 3 moderately well
Option 2 deals with Need 1 poorly, Need 2 moderately well and Need 4
    quite well.

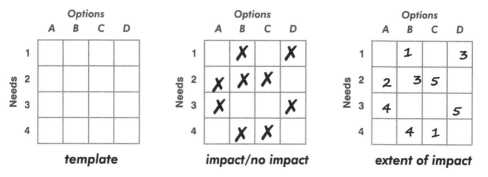

Figure 7.5 Relationship or Impact Matrix – Exploring the Options to Meet the Needs.

Option 3 deals with Need 2 fully and Need 4 poorly.
Option 4 deals with Need 1 moderately well and Need 3 fully.

The example highlights several interesting points:

1   It is not always possible to have a single option that deals with all the needs,
2   various options may deliver various levels of effectiveness,
3   some options can be immediately disregarded and
4   even a simple project to reduce waste is rarely that straightforward in the
    real world.

Now you have list of options that, together, can deliver all the needs; you
just need to select the optimal combination that provides the most effective
delivery, right? Well, no, there are still other issues to take into account.
These can include available budget, time and resources as well as skills and
capabilities.

When do options become solutions? The seriously nerdy answer is when
it is adopted as the way forward for implementation. A reality check will tell
you that most people use these terms interchangeably. So a sensible time is after the brainstorming and/or after a Fishbone analysis when the options have
been subject to some discussion and have some outcome parameters attached
to them, as described in the next section.

Planning and implementing an improvement project

In the previous chapter, I discussed how we identify the Most Likely Cause
and the Root Cause. These technical causes, and the list of optimal options
we have just developed, all need to be in a shape or form that everyone can
understand – What are we trying to achieve? And how will we achieve that?
It is about putting some more details on the list of possible options and also
ensuring that the options themselves are easy, simple and practical.

To do this, we need to revisit the Criticality Assessment. What is critical to the success of the improvement? There are many ways to carry out the Criticality Assessment; it can be quite intuitive: you will know readily what can impact a successful implementation in a day-to-day situation. The thing to remember is to make sure you do not miss out anything, and this is where an enquiry framework can help you – the Balanced Scorecard, the Triple Bottom Line and others are all designed to be comprehensive, and they can help you cover the relevant Criticality parameters (Figure 7.6).

You may wish to explore other frameworks such as the 4Ps or the SWOT (Strengths, Weaknesses, Opportunities and Threats) model (Table 7.1). The 4Ps (or the Marketing Mix[6]) has the four following perspectives, which we can use in a Criticality analysis as

The Classic 5 Questions Cluster

Once you have compiled your list of Criticalities, you can start to put together a project plan. A quick way to do this is to ask five questions: the classic What/How/Who/When/Why cluster. If you ask these questions in a particular

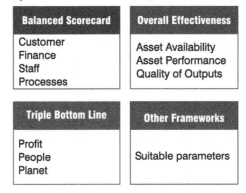

Assessing Criticalities
- Suggested Procedure

1) Select Framework (see examples below):

Balanced Scorecard	Overall Effectiveness
Customer Finance Staff Processes	Asset Availability Asset Performance Quality of Outputs

Triple Bottom Line	Other Frameworks
Profit People Planet	Suitable parameters

2) Ask:
I) How can this parameter impact on a successful project?
   List all practical ways this can impact on the project
ii) How significant is each impact? (1=Low, 5=High)

3) Analyse:
I) Examine the high impact issues
ii) What needs to be done to address these issues?

Figure 7.6 Assessing Criticalities.

way and in a particular order, you will develop a very straightforward outline project plan. This, the Classic 5 Questions Cluster,[8] is shown in Figure 7.7. This area is also discussed in some detail in Chapter 8 and Figure 8.10.

• The What and How questions and their answers form the project objectives and implementation approach;
• The Who and When questions and answers deal with the resources and timetable; and
• The Why question reminds every one of the benefits from the project.

With the general methodology outlined by the How question, you can also set performance measures based on the chosen method and link achievements to timetable details from the When question.

Table 7.1 Deploying the Marketing Mix Model

Perspective	*Conventional Use in Marketing*	*As a Framework for Criticality Assessment*
Product	Define the product/service	List what performance qualities are necessary to make product/service delivery a success
Place	Where to access the product/service	Identify the locations that can affect a successful delivery
Price	What is the actual/Switching Cost	Examine the estimated cost[7] of a successful delivery
Promotion	How shall we tell people of the product/service	Explore how we communicate the project plan/targets/progress to our intended audience

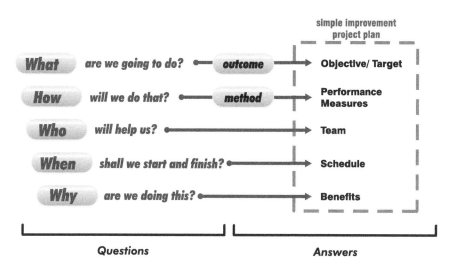

Figure 7.7 The Classic 5 Questions Cluster.

Table 7.2 Presenting a Problem or Presenting a Solution

A Traditional Scene	A Classic 5 Questions Cluster Scene
Team: Boss, we have a problem. XYZ doesn't work? What do you want us to do? Boss: I am very busy right now, see me later.	Team: Boss, we have a problem. XYZ doesn't work, but we have a suggestion: This is what we have to do to fix it ... This is how we will do it ... We can start tomorrow morning and be finished by midday ... We will need Mike to help us here ... The benefits are as follows ... Boss: I am very busy right now, but this sounds right, go for it...

The Classic 5 Questions Cluster is often sufficient for simple projects that involve a few people at a specific work location or for a particular work procedure. This is an approach I used extensively during the team workshops at the London Olympic construction when I ask a team to explore improvements. After they came up with an improvement idea, I then guided them through the five questions to help them firm up their idea in a practical way. It was also very useful when they then explained to their manager what they are suggesting, as shown in Table 7.2.

This is a positive approach towards the initial reporting and solving of a problem. I recommend this because it helps build team confidence and can also transform the relationship dynamics between a team and its manager towards respect and trust.

For anything more detailed than a starting discussion or a more detailed issue, the 5 Questions model needs to be reinforced with more detailed analysis, discussion and perhaps consultation. Nonetheless, for a quick explanation to the boss, to stakeholders or to the media, the 5 Questions is a useful tool.

Extending the What/How relationships

The options have now been put into context and ideally simplified and made easy to operate with the 5 Questions model to provide a straightforward framework towards detailed planning. The next step is extending the analysis from the Needs/Options matrix in Figure 7.5. This extends the What/How relationship described in Chapter 4 and Figure 4.10.

If you examine the Options (or Hows), you will find that they are actually defining a new level of Needs: What do we need to do to deliver these methods/performance measures? This is then cascaded further to a new set of Options (Hows). Why are we doing this? Well, it helps us define the process better and gives us an idea of the efforts, people and the costs required. This is shown in Figure 7.8.[9]

Extending the What/ How relationships
- getting to the next level of Needs/ Options

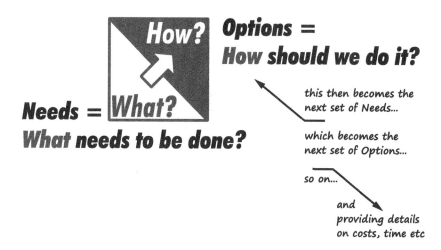

Figure 7.8 Extending the What/How Relationship.

Developing a project plan

There are a very large number of textbooks on project management and project planning, as well as advanced project management frameworks such as PRINCE 2, PMBOK and Agile.[10] For our purposes, I am suggesting the same approach from Chapter 6 – the backwards approach based on What/ How.

> What is the *final* outcome of the project?
> How will we get there?

A more technical way (i.e. using jargon) of explaining at the backwards approach is "Pull." In Lean jargon, this means being "pulled by the customer's needs" rather than being "pushed by the supplier's needs."[11] In plain language, this is about delivering value to the customer or end user – the value being what they want and not just what will benefit us. I discussed this in Chapter 6 – see Figure 6.4.

By examining "how will we get there," we can establish the previous step and so on. However, it is important to note that in using this technique, you are focussing solely on the activities that achieve the outcome operationally. You will need to add value-enabling elements such as governance, training or communications as well as any legal compliance elements. The result-driven or customer pull methodology provides not just a skeletal project

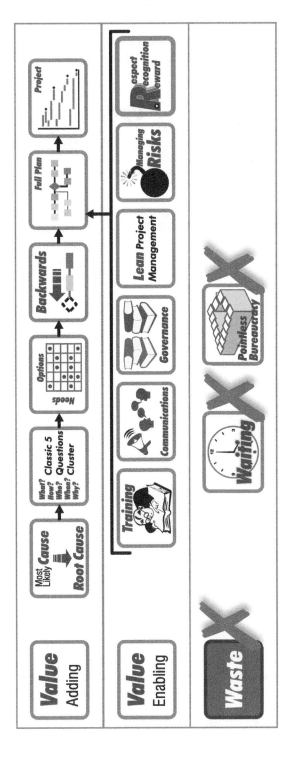

Figure 7.9 Result–Driven Project Planning.

plan but also uses the criticalities to add the details, such as training, communication, reporting, project management, risks management and rewards. Figure 7.9 outlines the various components of this approach to project planning.

Lean project management

Many projects do not work out, and they end up costing a lot more money, not realising the full benefits and perhaps embarrassing people[12] for a number of reasons, such as overambitious targets, poor project management and poor communications. For projects to improve Energy Productivity, you do not want the bad reputation a project failure can bring, as that can discredit all the other good ideas you are planning to put forward. Don't be pessimistic, however; there are ways to minimise the risks of failure. The most straightforward way is to ask "what can go wrong?"; to identify the potential problem areas and then deal with them either by designing them out of the project plan or by designing mitigation into the plan (to refresh your memory on these topics, have a look at Figure 6.2).

A potential problem or a risk is simply something that *can* go wrong, but hasn't (yet). This can include minor events such as printers running out of toner at the critical time or the departure of a senior team member to a competitor. In many cases, we usually have an idea of what may go wrong in a project, and these are often issues with people, time, external dependencies, processes, knowledge and budget. The categorisation is useful to identify the possible problems and deal with them in a structured manner. You can also assess the Criticality of the potential problems and rank their impacts.

A suggested approach to minimise these potential problems or issues is to adopt a Lean attitude towards project planning and look at ways to minimise problems and optimise project flow. There are two streams of actions in this approach: exploring potential problems in the draft plan and using past experience and data to help avoid these in the planned project, as shown in Figure 7.10. One of the ways that potential problems can be explored is by using project modelling, such as the Building Information Modelling (BIM) I described in Chapter 5.

Past data and personal experience are useful because they reflect how your organisation dealt with such issues historically and offer a guide on how similar actions in your organisation may result in similar outcomes in the future as well. This is partly a reflection on the culture and procedures of your organisation and also the capabilities and characteristics of your colleagues.

The aim of the Lean project approach is to design out potential problems as much as possible or to reduce or mitigate the impacts of those that cannot be designed out. You can apply this to both the Value Adding and Value Enabling parts of the improvement project. By identifying these potential and past trouble spots, you can rank them for their respective impact and plan accordingly.

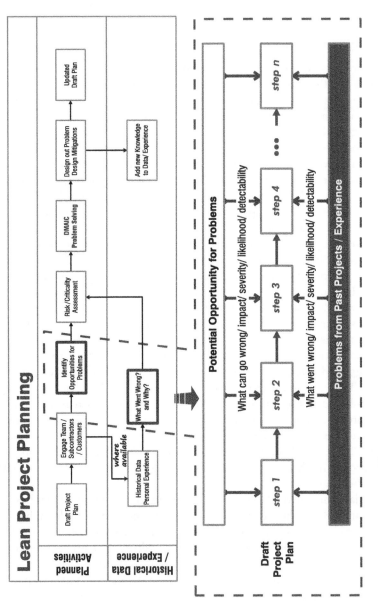

Figure 7.10 Lean Project Planning.

The analysis I recommend is the FMEA method described in Chapter 4 (see Figure 4.11). I choose this method because of the two useful variables from the analysis: the likelihood of the risk and the detectability of the risk. Likelihood is straightforward but allows us to rank the risk of the particular problem. Detectability brings us to a different area of risk management: If we cannot easily detect the problem, can we assume everything is okay? It is like having a slow leak in a car tyre or slow leak in a water tank kept in a cupboard. Detectability is not just the ease of detecting something, it is also about the unknowns. In terms of what can go wrong, you can have four categories: the known and unknown risks as well as the known and unknown impacts.[13] Segmenting into these four possibilities can help us determine how we deal with potential problems. Figure 7.11 offers a possible range of responses.

Designing out or mitigating **known risks and impacts** is a reasonably conventional approach to adopt and ideally should be common practice in organisations.

We use insurance to cover **unknown risks and known impacts** and sometimes we plan mitigations for these too: think about our holidays and our alternative plans on a potentially rainy day trip.

Known risks and unknown impacts are a different situation – just like before the Brexit referendum, companies, government and individuals were making preparations ranging from exploring office space in Europe to people changing their pound sterling to euros. It is all about being prepared and ready. But how do you develop readiness in a corporate context? And how do you know that the contents of your readiness training are in the right ballpark?

Readiness is not about having endless fire drills, but rather about cultivating a sense of responsibility in the workforce. Prepare them to be ready

Figure 7.11 Knowns and Unknowns.

by letting your staff have a sense of the bigger picture of the company; offer them some responsibility and accountability about their work areas as well as delegating sufficient authority (coupled with the right training) such that an unexpected problem can be dealt with through pragmatic or innovative solutions.

Unknown risks and unknown impacts are difficult to describe, as we do not know what we do not know! However, instances of tsunamis, major earthquakes or other catastrophes (the real kind, not the ones often announced in the media as catastrophes – such as when a performer cancelled a concert) generally bring unknown impacts.

The impacts are unknown because they are usually more than just a disrupted business or supply chain, as they can include loss of lives as well as the efforts needed to overcome the shock of the event. Often the unknown is the scale of the catastrophe – the Somerset Levels in England suffers regular flooding, but the flood of 2014 was significantly worse than anyone expected. It is usually the severity of the impacts from unknown risks that can cause shock and possibly a paralysis in responding. Lesser calamities, such as transport strikes, are also difficult to manage, as this can mean your critical staff just cannot get to work.[14]

Unfortunately, there is not a lot you can do to prevent these in a corporate sense. Realistic responses in the early days after a natural disaster are often about resilience of the surviving corporate framework and how well the organisation prepared itself. In some ways, acceptance of the unexpected catastrophe is about all many organisations can do.

Improvement – integrating technology, people and process

Any improvement project, whether it is a technology improvement project, a people-centred initiative or a process improvement, will need to contain similar components: There will be a need for communications to market the project, and there will also be a need for training to help the staff involved such that they can deliver the results optimally. These actions are summarised in Figure 7.12.

The communications and marketing elements in Figure 7.12 are really about what you say (the communications) and how you say it (the marketing). These comprise four main pieces of information and how this information is packaged:

- Activities: a description of what is to be done
- Timetable: the sequence and schedule of the activities
- Reason: the benefits to be gained or the waste to be reduced
- Context: this is the packaging or the marketing to ensure the information is easy/simple/practical to the people receiving it.

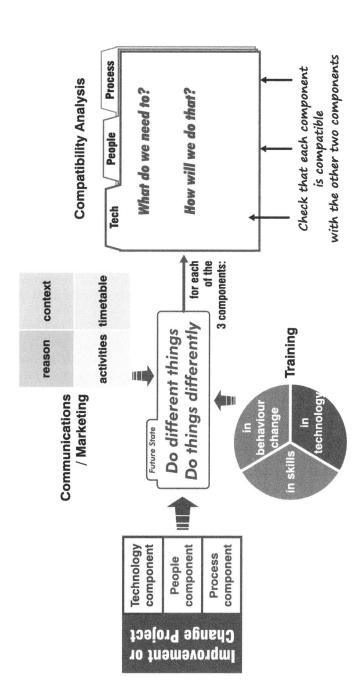

Figure 7.12 Designing for Improvement/Change.

The training elements in Figure 7.12 are there to make sure that people actually know what they are required to do and (hopefully) able to carry out the activities correctly. Therefore, the three training elements are

- Technology: to use it directly to add value, to use it to control or monitor the process, to use it to analyse the outputs
- Skills: to operate the technology, to operate the Future State process, to act or behave in a way that results in delivering the Future State
- Behaviour change: to optimise technology deployment and operation, to optimise in operating process

The analysis is based on the What/How analysis, except that there is an additional compatibility analysis for the three components: technology/people/process.

The compatibility analysis

You may have the best marketing and training initiatives but if these cannot integrate the technology, people and process components, then your initiatives may not go too well, as this may leave people with confused messages and conflicting opinions on what to do.

We need to explore the improvement or change project on two levels – the value adding and the value enabling. Value adding is about the actual change or improvement: Do the three components interact in a value adding way? Value enabling is when one or two components are supporting the main focus – the value-adding activities. I suggest, therefore, that the training and communications/marketing elements in Figure 7.12 can be seen as value enabling.

For example, to make sure a new process fully realises its potential, a company decides to introduce a different calibration/monitoring regime (technology-related). To make sure that the calibration/ monitoring is carried out effectively, the company decides to introduce a new lighting system. Thus far, the actions are compatible. However, the company also decides that the staff's well being can also enhance its productivity and therefore also improve its catering provisions (people-related). This enhancement activity is neutral to the lighting enhancement and the new calibration regime, and the discrete activities can appear not linked.

As such, the company may need to pay attention to how it communicates these changes. Will it appear too manipulative if it directly links better catering to enhance motivation towards monitoring? Will it instead go for a generally "we care about your wellbeing message?"

Compatible options offer synergy of varying degree, whereas options neutral to each other may require some re-examination. Although these do not conflict, the entirely unconnected activities may cause confusion if people are looking at a cohesive set of integrated activities.

Sometimes you may have activities that are lightly linked (i.e. slightly incompatible) or totally not linked (i.e. incompatible) activities. In these instances, to avoid confusion and conflicts, you may need to accept the following ways forward: redesign, reschedule or abandon one or more actions. None of these choices are ideal, as they may delay or reduce the full realisation of the expected benefits. If these must be introduced, see whether it is possible to introduce them in phases such that any potential clashes are minimised.

Integrating technology, behaviour and processes is a good example of Do Things Differently or Do Different Things, or change. Managing change is a major element in Everyday Sustainability and improving Energy Productivity. While there are bookshelves full of books focussing on change management, let us nonetheless have a quick look at how to get along when technology, behaviour and processes change, individually or collectively.

You may wish to explore Appendix 3 for a more detailed look at analysing for compatibility among multiple options.

Change!

First, it is worth noting that things do not always happen all at once; people will take time to adapt to new or changing technologies, behaviours and processes. Therefore, we need to think about the level of capability we want our people to develop. Figure 7.13 shows a pathway that takes us from knowing very little about something different to becoming innovators in the same area. Table 7.3 illustrates the different stages of developing capability.

Do Different Things / Doing Things Differently
An novice-to-expert pathway

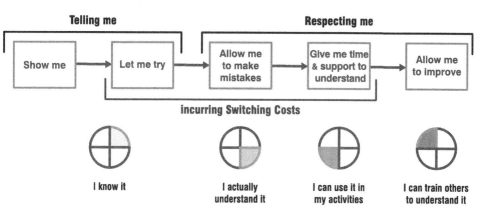

Based on a model by P. willmott

Figure 7.13 Do Different Things/Doing Things Differently – a Pathway.

Table 7.3 Developing Capacity – the Details

Stages	My Capabilities
Show me	I may remember some of it but likely to interpret it wrong or do it wrong.
Let me try	I have a better idea of what to do when supervised, but my confidence is not very high.
Allow me to make mistakes	Learning from my mistakes without repercussions is a good way to build my knowledge and confidence.
Give me time and support to understand	Rushing puts pressure on me, and errors can creep in. Giving me time to understand and practise builds my confidence and capability.
Allow me to improve	Ownership is achieved with confidence, and Switching Costs are minimised, since I am now part of the change/ improvement process.

Note: The Stages in Table 7.3 came from my colleague, Peter Willmott.

When we are dealing with change, we are talking about essentially two types of activity (Figure 7.14):

- Do Things Differently; or
- Do Different Things

Each of these addresses different needs. For example, in process improvement, workplace organisation usually means doing (similar) things differently, whereas a process improvement can be doing different things. A new process is more likely to be both doing things differently and doing different things. Note that I am talking about work at the process and procedure level, rather than at the strategic level. At higher levels, the abstraction can mean a new process is doing things differently if the outcome is still the same. However, one thing remains constant at whatever level or whichever sort of change – there is likely to be a Switching Cost. This is the cost associated with changing from one mode of operations to another.[15]

Do things differently

When only one of the three components of technology, people or process is value adding, then the situation is likely to be one of a "different way of

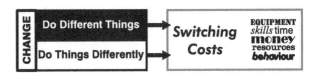

Figure 7.14 Change and the Switching Costs.

Table 7.4 Different Way of Working

Value-Adding Focus	Value-Enabling Areas	Outcome Example
Technology	People	Update skills: improve productivity
	Process	Update process: optimise efficiency
People	Technology	Update technology: exploit new features
	Process	Update process: increase productivity
Process	Technology	Update technology: optimise performance
	People	Update skills: increase effectiveness

working." This is probably more readily encountered in organisations where continuous improvement is being carried out. In these cases, the relationships and the outcomes can be summarised in Table 7.4.

The Energy Productivity implications are quite clear when the value-adding focus and value-enabling actions are reviewed together. It is necessary for the value-enabling actions to be coordinated effectively if we are to realise the benefits of the improvement. Table 7.4 can be used to illustrate the negatives when the enabling actions are not coordinated effectively. All the "improve/optimise/exploit" options become wasted or benefits not (fully) realised.

Do different things

This situation means that instead of "updating," the enabling actions are likely to be "learning" or "introducing." Both of these are likely to require more time and effort than updating existing practice or knowledge.

- Different technology often has a tendency to not work as well as expected, partly because it is not familiar and partly because it may not have been optimised for the particular working environment.
- Different behaviour, whether in working or in general, is hard to adopt because people often find change more difficult than they first thought.
- Different process means learning new technology/techniques and developing new behaviour. Although a different process or procedure often has similar outcomes (but better implemented), there will always be a cost to changing in terms of effort and time.

The Switching Costs[16]

Switching Costs are the tangible and intangible costs of changing from one approach/behaviour/technology to another. You can consider the Switching Costs issues by asking "what will make it difficult to switch?" With the subsequent list of barriers and potential barriers, comes a set of requirements to overcome, and these can then be assessed through a cascading What/How Matrix analysis as shown in Figure 7.8.

The options should provide a path towards minimising or managing the Switching Costs. This can include redesign, changed timetable as well as further investment in training and carrying out an effective communications programme.

Lowering the Switching Costs barrier

There may be many elements to consider in lowering the Switching Costs, and one simple way to explore these is to use an adapted Fishbone analysis. Instead of looking for causes of problems, as described in Chapter 6, the aim here is to find ways forward. Figure 7.15 shows how this can be constructed using a few common factors that can help lower the Switching Costs. As in any Fishbone analysis, you can choose the factors that are most relevant in your situation. It does not need to have six factors if four will do.

The aim of this analysis is to list the activities that can help reduce the Switching Costs; these can come from the result of a brainstorming session with the actions being grouped into each of the factors, as explained in Chapter 6. This then becomes the requirements of a What/How Matrix analysis, and you can then explore the options to go forward. The type of questions to ask, to start the analysis, are shown on Table 7.5.

Integrating technology, behaviour and process is not a particularly easy task, but it is not impossible either. It does, however, require some detailed planning and meticulous dialogues to ensure people are onboard. This is not just to minimise the initial Switching Costs, but also to embed the new practices and habits in such a way as to prevent the benefits from being eroded in future years by people slipping back into previous practices.

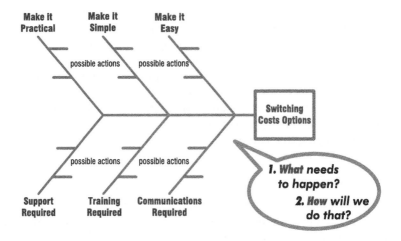

Figure 7.15 Easing the Switching Costs – Adapting the Fishbone Analysis.

Table 7.5 Question Time

Factors	Examples of Questions to Ask
Make it easy	Technology: Is the technology difficult to use or not well understood? Behaviour: Can we introduce the change bit by bit? Process: Is this easy to work in our working environment?
Make it simple	Technology: Is it complicated to learn or operate? Behaviour: What are we really looking for? Process: Can we split any long/complex steps?
Make it practical	Technology: Can our people understand the instructions? Behaviour: Can we make it difficult to get it wrong? Process: Does this make sense to our people?
Communications needed	Technology: Can we explain and demystify? Behaviour: Can we encourage participation, respect and recognise effort? Process: Can we outline clearly the benefits to everyone?
Training needed	Technology: Is our training fit for purpose? Behaviour: How do we encourage participation? Process: Can we set up pilots and encourage discussions?
Support needed	Technology: How do we help our people who couldn't cope? Behaviour: How do we help our people who couldn't cope? Process: How do we help our people who couldn't cope?

We have explored how to set up an improvement initiative; now we look at how to keep it on track and not slip backwards.

Controlling the *gains*

This is one of the biggest issues with improvement projects – when, after all the effort, the organisation slips backwards to previous practices. This is not about missing the short-term targets; it is about maintaining them in the medium to long term. The good news is that if you followed suggestions such as those in this book, reverting to the previous situations are less likely. The bad news, however, is that you cannot merely sit back and live happily ever after. Successful *gains* in Overall Effectiveness and Energy Productivity need to be nurtured and maintained. Figure 7.16 describes some of the factors that will require attention.

Why do people and organisations slip back to the old ways? Sometimes it is because people become bored, or the new approach did not deliver the promised results, or the organisation decided the "job's done" and slacked off. It may also be because management attention slipped, perhaps the rewards were not distributed evenly, or the new approach hit snags, or the company changed its focus and so on. While it is feasible to rerun the improvement initiative,[17] it is more difficult to rebuild the motivation and enthusiasm. Let's look at the possible causes in some detail to see how the "recidivism" comes about.

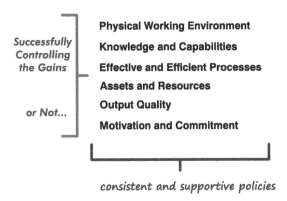

Figure 7.16 Energy Productivity Success Factors.

Bored – People get bored when there is nothing interesting happening. Just about everyone can be enthused about a new initiative, but if there is no ownership by the workforce, then there is little to keep the excitement going. If the new approach is entirely top down with little workforce engagement, or the improvement project was run by consultants, then after the initial excitement wears off, common reactions can include picking faults or making trouble. Proverbs like "idle hands are the devil's workshop" often have some grains of truth in them.

Did not deliver – This can be because of poor planning, inadequate skills or over-promising by the project sponsor. Poor or weak planning happens perhaps because we did not make plans in the right context or we just got it wrong totally. Over-promising is rather different: People over-promise because they want to sell their idea or product. Management may over-promise to gain the staff's support. This is not necessarily malicious or deliberate; people may also over-promise or over-sell because they genuinely believe it will deliver more.

Job's done – Many organisations reckon that improvement actions are a one-off, and thereafter their attention turns to the next management fad. Or they have achieved the initial success and thought thereafter the good life will be perpetual. Anyone on the project team who wants to continue under these circumstances is likely to find disinterest from the organisation.

Not paying attention – Business takes place in a dynamic realm, and managers usually have many other things to deal with. If the initial implementation seems to be running well, attention can then be shifted to the next issue/crisis.

Rewards? What rewards? – Sometimes the efforts, achievements and rewards are not balanced or perceived to be unfair. Thereafter, the "why bother" mentality takes over and cynicism spreads. Designing an effective rewards system is discussed in greater detail in Chapter 10.

Snags – Things may just go wrong or not work out as planned. Perhaps the training was not right, or the new technology is more complex than first thought, or the process is too abstract. Or it can just be bad luck.[18] The rising number of problems can quickly erode confidence in the improvement initiative.

Company changes focus – This is similar to the "job's done" situation, but on a corporate level, and then it becomes very hard to move against the overall corporate momentum; but Everyday Sustainability should not go off the corporate agenda if it is saving money and doing good.

One way to tackle these issues is to use the Play-Do-Check-Act (PDCA) continuous improvement cycle, as shown in Figure 7.17. This is a familiar tool for quality improvement, but we are using it for controlling the *gains* and therefore the focus is not just on improvements, but also on how we can maintain and grow the benefits from the improvement.

Plan – As normal but look at ways in which can make continuous improvement easier. This can include a policy to encourage experimentation in everyday tasks. Many world-class companies, such as 3M or Google, offer their staff time every month to carry out improvement projects.[19]

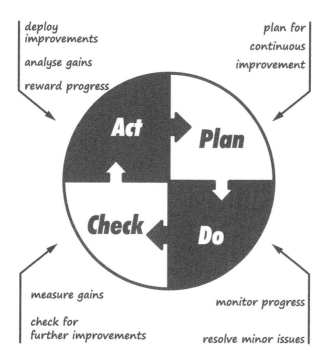

Figure 7.17 Using the Continuous Improvement Cycle to Control *Gains*.

Do – This is when the implementation happens and progress is monitored. This is also when people notice that the plans were not perfect, and small (or larger) issues crop up. With sufficient delegated authority, the frontline teams involved in the improvement should be able to resolve many of these issues on-the-job. Nonetheless, the more detailed or complex ideas should be held back until the next improvement phrase to avoid disruption to the operations.

Check – Has the improvement achieved its targets? The *gains* are measured and any ideas for further improvements logged. This is where the frontline teams can see their ideas adopted (and adapted) for piloting or rolling out. It is probably the easiest way to keeping people engaged and interested.

Act – This is when the new improvements are implemented and when rewards are given. Again, this action encourages engagement and keeps interest at a sufficiently high level towards the next PDCA cycle.

In the PDCA cycle, it is assumed that there is always adequate and appropriate training, as well as communications. Communications is a major part of maintaining interest and engagement in the organisation, and it needs to be both upwards and downwards within the hierarchy (and across if you work in a matrix organisation!). Beyond communications, there needs to be a delegated authority and a responsibility regime for continuous improvement at the working level.

At the top, there needs to be a champion with sufficient knowledge and interest to help push Energy Productivity innovations along. S/he does not need to be a specialist other than having expertise in removing barriers.

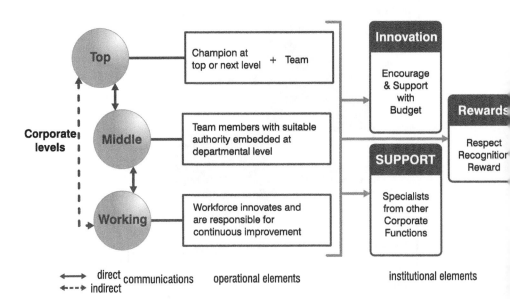

Figure 7.18 Controlling the *Gains* – Framework and Support System.

While the corporate support functions such as Finance, Human Resources or Legal can offer their specialist knowledge to help with the continuous improvement, it does not always work because of the poor reputation these functions may have.[20] However, a capable and respected leader in these functions can make partnership a reality.

At the working level, the individuals and teams will have noticed small issues which they can fix immediately, but they may also come up with ways of "doing it better." These should be collected and put into the Check and Act stages. This allows empowerment and ownership but within a fixed framework (and should reassure all the more traditional stakeholders).

Between the top and the working levels, managers need to engage in dialogue both up and down the organisation as well as act as a channel to provide extra support from specialists and facilitate innovation.

Figure 7.18 shows the framework for controlling the *gains*.

This chapter looked at how to integrate technology, behaviour and process management to carry out Everyday Sustainability and improve Energy Productivity through eliminating process problems and enhancing process efficiency. The aims need to include ways to make sure that the *gains* from an improvement programme are not eroded. But how do we get to this point? The next few chapters look at the roles of the Boss as well as ways of selling the idea of Energy Productivity to the various stakeholders in the first place.

Notes

1 It is not a theoretical solution since the solution is derived with data from the *gemba* and involved facts and analysis that conform to the technical and logical reality of the workplace. The real world tends to have less logic and more chaos, confusion and emotions.

2 Even McDonald's, the globalised burger chain, has localised menu items such as shrimp burgers for the Far East, salmon burgers in Scandinavia and other products designed for local palates around the world.

3 Even the servers at the restaurants are not too good at this; if you ask what is the third item on the list of specials, chances are you'll get the entire recitation again.

4 Quality people do one better; they called these options "Substitute Quality Characteristics"!

5 The Impact Matrix and its cousins are described in detail in Chapter 9.

6 See Appendix 2 for more details, and don't forget, the name of the tool does not restrict it to any specific use; it is how you use it to inform and make decisions that matters.

7 The costs include the tangible costs in cash, time etc. and also the intangible "switching" cost of behaviour; more on that in the following pages.

8 Also see my book on sustainable construction: No Waste, Gower 2011.

9 This concept is extrapolated much, much further in Appendix 3 and Figure A3.19.

10 If your employer wants you to use these, they will put you on special courses to get trained and perhaps certificated.

11 Toyota has a more complex way of explaining Pull, but for most daily situations, the simple, easy and practical explanation here works just as well. See Appendix 2 for more details.

12 See Endnote 2 in Chapter 3 about the UK National Health Service IT programme and its travails.
13 Donald Rumsfeld, former US Defense Secretary said in 2002 "... there are known knowns; there are things we know we know. We also know there are known unknowns; that is to say we know there are some things we do not know. But there are also unknown unknowns - the ones we don't know we don't know..." and now, you know (I think...).
14 Sometimes it is not necessarily a strike that causes delays; on 8 May 2017, a herd of llamas wandered onto train lines in Southeast England (I kid you not), resulting in delays of people getting to work: "Boss, I'm going to be late because there's a herd of llamas blocking the track..."
15 Actually, it is not just for changes in operations – even when you change shoes there is a bit of getting used to the different pair – an everyday Switching Cost.
16 See also Appendix 2.
17 And consultants will love you for this, as they get paid again.
18 Perhaps, but as Arnold Palmer, the famous golfer, said: "the more I practice, the luckier I get".
19 In a 2013 London Business School report, Julian Birkinshaw reported that 3M pioneered the notional 15 per cent innovation time, and Google offered 20 per cent "innovation time off".
20 In a certain university, which has to remain nameless, the HR and Finance functions usually vie for the position of being the second-least popular with the university staff. Suffice to say that instead of thinking how to offer real improvements in their service, these two groups spend their time thinking up superficial changes to compete for the coveted second-last spot.

8   The Boss' Action Plan

Before we get to stakeholders, let's have a quick look at the Boss' role first.

The aims of the Boss' Action Plan are to enable and engender the transformation from a less effective Current State to a more optimised Future State. In other words, to move from the four possible negatives from a poorly managed Current State to four preferred positives at a Future State, graphically described in Figure 8.1.

Now, as the boss or a senior executive, you have colleagues suggesting that you should consider Everyday Sustainability as well as measuring the Energy Productivity Key Performance Indicator (KPI) for your organisation/team. That all sounds pretty good (trust me, it is!), but you need to go through a bit of analysis yourself before coming to a decision. What do you need to

Figure 8.1 Improvements – Current to Future State.

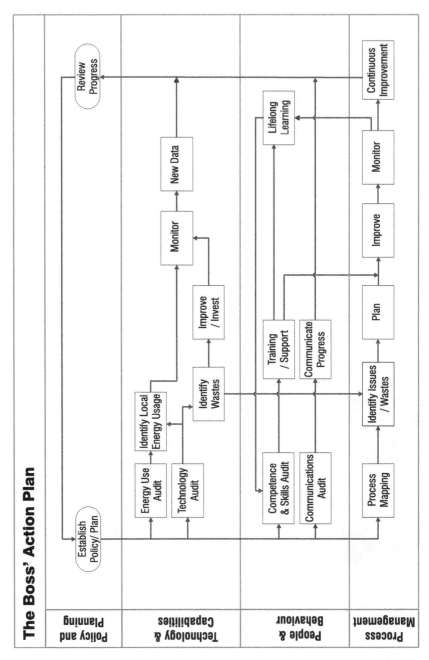

Figure 8.2 The Boss' Action Plan.

find out about your organisation? About your team? Internal and external conditions? And of course, what's in it for you and what do you actually need to do? The next section looks at these areas and helps you collate the necessary information to form a decision.

A Swim Lane description of The Boss' Action Plan is shown in Figure 8.2. Now be aware that many bosses will be too busy to do this her/himself, but will instead appoint a project manager to do the (donkey) work.

The Action Plan is divided into the three Everyday Sustainability areas of Technology and Capabilities; People and Behaviour; and Process Management, together with an overall policy and planning. Figure 8.2 shows that this Action Plan is a repeating cycle in the form of a Plan—Do—Check—Act (PDCA) continuous improvement cycle, with the three action components taking place concurrently. As these are mutually dependent, there needs to be adequate and appropriate communications between them.

The activities of the Action Plan are all described in various sections of this book.

Not the boss (yet)?

And if you are not (yet) the boss, this approach can also help you prepare your proposal or business case by answering some questions the boss may have on these areas! These questions are often in the form of: "What can these activities do for us?" then "How can we make that happen?" or "What are the risks?" followed by "And what can we do about them?"

I suggest you consider using conventional business analysis frameworks to help answer these questions. Two examples are described in Figures 8.3 and 8.4, respectively.

Both these models have a number of areas to depict a balanced management model, but the questions remain the same.

In the analysis part, you can readily answer by either using real numbers (£/\$/€/¥) or assigning relative outcomes of 1 to 5 with 1 being low and 5 being high.

The plan for going forward is a What/How analysis expanded to asking five simple questions, as shown in Figure 8.5.

Answering these five questions gives an outline action plan. While this is likely to impress your boss and score you kudos points, it is not yet a fully realised plan, but instead a starting point for more detailed analysis and planning (such as that described in Chapter 10). Some of the issues raised from the analysis in Figures 8.3 and 8.4 may also need more detailed assessment than the simple outline shown above.

In Chapter 6, I described the Define, Measure, Analyse, Improve and Control (DMAIC) problem-solving process, and here we use a modified version, which has a more intensive Identification element in the Define phase,

Extended Triple Bottom Line*
Analysis and Planning

Analysis (for each area):

1. *Define the situation you want to assess*
2. *Then ask "Is there any value added in these areas?"; and*
3. *"If no value added, is there any waste?"*

Action Planning (for each area):

1. *What shall we do to achieve/ prevent this?*
2. *How will we do that?*

* Source: No Waste, Ma
  Original Triple Bottom Line, Elkington, 1994;

Figure 8.3 Extended Triple Bottom Line.

Extended Balanced Scorecard*
Analysis and Planning

Analysis (for each area):

1. *Define the situation you want to assess*
2. *Then ask "Is there any value added in these areas?"; and*
3. *"If no value added, is there any waste?"*

Action Planning (for each area):

1. *What shall we do to achieve/ prevent this?*
2. *How will we do that?*

* Original Balanced Scorecard, Kaplin and Norton, 1992

Figure 8.4 Extended Balanced Scorecard*.

Going Forward
From the What/ How analysis to a Simple Action Plan

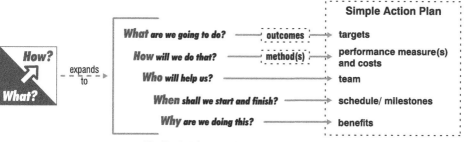

Figure 8.5 Analysis and Planning.

Table 8.1 SWOT and PEST Analysis[1]

Internal Factors (SWOT Analyses)[2]	*External Factors (PEST Analysis)[2]*
Strengths – what we are good at	Political – generally legal and tax, as well as political stability, rule of law etc.
Weaknesses – what we are less good at	Economic – the overall economic sentiment – locally, regionally, globally
Opportunities – what our strengths let us exploit	Social – cultural trends, can be linked to the two elements above
Threats – the events our weaknesses will expose us to	Technological – what changes can impact us and how they can change our business model

as you may need to defend your proposed changes or improvements at a more strategic level.

The Identification process is therefore made up of several activities, starting with a survey of the business environment, both internal and external, of your organisation. To make life easier for ourselves, I suggest we use simple, well-understood analytical tools, as shown in Table 8.1.

After establishing the internal and external factors that drive your corporate direction, it is time to see whether the organisation is dysfunctional in its activities. Signs of poor management can act as a mirror to the way the organisation functions. Poor management can be divided into four broad categories:[3]

- **Incompetence** – cannot deliver, lead or manage
- **Over-reaching** – too ambitious and disregarding the organisation's capabilities and processes in setting targets

- **Perversity** – going for the non-sensible, irrational, impractical or pointless activities; have a "not invented here" attitude; and close-minded to new ideas. Glory seeking/ego tripping can also be seen as signs of perversity as can idiosyncrasy.
- **Inconsistency** – changing directions according to whim/fashion, driven by personality not rules and focussed on chasing short-term targets

(By the way, do these four categories remind you of some current world leaders?)

A good way to identify these is to do a quick check and go through the 10 Common Hidden Wastes described in Chapter 6. All ten hidden wastes can be manifested through the poor management categories of incompetence, over-reaching, perversity and inconsistency. The "Go and See" approach is also very appropriate here for senior people, as they can "go and see" the real situation at work and not rely on possibly biased information that may be filtered by their subordinates.

However, remember that many organisations suffer from the twin traps of "that's how we do thing here" thinking and the "we cannot change" pessimism. Therefore, be cautious when approaching these issues, but also be positive, as shown in a light-hearted fashion in Table 8.2.

Much of this type of response, light-heartedness notwithstanding, is about you being prepared to deal with awkward people and attitudes. Sucking up is not particularly comfortable to carry out, but if it gets an obstacle out of the way, how much has it cost you?[4]

Sometimes though, having a strong corporate culture (which can be seen as idiosyncratic or "how we do thing here") is fine as long as it adds value.

Possible examples of poor management, which can include treasured or historical corporate values, can again be assessed by using the Balanced Scorecard or the Triple Bottom Line frameworks to make sure they are adding value or not in a real-world environment. The critical action to check is whether the various identified examples of management creating waste in the organisation are analysed by the techniques shown in Figures 8.3 and 8.4.

Table 8.2 Smoke, Mirrors and Silver Tongue

From	To
"that's how we do things here"	We have done very well, and we are now leveraging our heritage/knowledge/ experience (take your pick as appropriate) to maintain our culture/ lead/way of doing thing
"we cannot change"	Well, yes, we have; you have shown us that we can change successfully (think of appropriate example, ideally from the past that nobody really remembers)

This point is to arrive at a quick analysis of a situation – Is there poor management? Does it result in wasted resources or no value added?

Once the poor management observations have been confirmed, then these become problems and are dealt with by using the DMAIC methodology, for example. However, in this instance, the DMAIC approach is looking at a more strategic-level issue and the impacts are likely to be more across the organisation than just one team.

Define – What is the problem? How did it come about? When/where did this problem first appear? The objective at this stage is to gather sufficient information for a detailed analysis. As these are likely to be strategic issues, both the problem and its solution may be more complex than the operational issues, as described in Chapter 6.

Measure – How serious is this problem? You need to select the parameters that reflect how your organisation measures success. The parameter can be anything, but it needs to be consistently applied to all the problems, and it also needs to be meaningful to the people making the decisions (including the boss). By comparing the various problems, you can then rank and prioritise them. The technique used to identify this is the Pareto Rule or the Lever Rule,[5] as shown in Figure 8.6.

Analyse – What is causing the poor management? This brings us back to the DMAIC analysis of finding the likely causes and the Root Cause.

Improve – When dealing with strategic directions for the company, this can become quite complex, but the description earlier in this chapter on developing the proposal will help you structure the implementation.

Control – This is a critical issue in looking at changing strategic directions towards Everyday Sustainability. The objective is not giving up or sliding back into old practices. Everyday Sustainability is not a fad for this year; it

Deploying the Pareto or Lever Rule

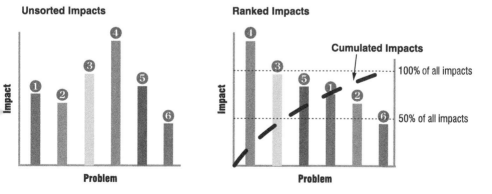

Figure 8.6 Going Forward – From the What/How Analysis to a Simple Action Plan.

is a way of working that links good sustainability outcomes with improved efficiency and effectiveness. So there is nothing to dislike, except perhaps the hard work in getting there.

Now, after you managed to get the top people on side, let's move on to getting the message out to everyone at work.

Notes

1 Also described in Chapter 6: Table 6.2 and Figure 6.3.
2 See Appendix 2.
3 These were adapted from B. Tuchman's, *The March of Folly*, Knopf, 1984.
4 Just remember this message on a fortune cookie: If you can fake sincerity, you've got it made!
5 Also known as the 80:20 rule, where 80 per cent of the impacts are caused by 20 per cent of the problems; see Appendix 2.

9 Selling it!

In principle, winning the hearts and minds should not be difficult with an initiative like Everyday Sustainability, since it is capable of addressing the needs of different groups: saving money, reducing waste, saving time, work-force ownership of new ideas, doing good and doing sustainability, as well as encouraging innovations. What's not to like?

The problem is that it is not always easy to sell a good deal. It is actually easier to sell a bad deal: You can utilise people's greed or laziness to encourage them to accept the deal, and these can be supplemented by marketing hype, blinding people with (pseudo) science or with outright lies.[1] And in times of uncertainty, the promises from the lies usually sound better.

But offering something that's good for you? Well, the sale is much harder, partly because we can't really lie about it, but principally, it is because there is always some effort involved, as shown in Table 9.1. Whatever lever we use to

Table 9.1 Benefits and Efforts

Benefits/Levers	Efforts Required
Save money	Carry out analysis, solve problems, implement improvement, monitor, control gains and behaviour change
Save time	Analyse wasted time, develop solutions and engage staff in discussion, implement improvement, encourage good practice, reward success and behaviour change
Raise quality	Carry out Plan-Do-Check-Act quality improvement process repeatedly, adopt as part of everyday activity and behaviour change
Engage staff	Carry out analysis, solve problems, implement improvement, monitor and control gains as well as really listening
Innovations	Create suitable environment, budget time and money, accept initial failures and slow start, persevere, share rewards
Raise productivity	Analyse activities, solve problems, behaviour change, manage risks and share rewards
Do everyday sustainability	Break down silo thinking, introduce partnerships at work and invest time, effort and money to keep it going as well as report progress, gains and share rewards (and behaviour change, of course)

attract people to the benefits of an enhanced Energy Productivity, the efforts required cannot be hidden.

From this angle, offering a good deal seems to require relentless toil; endless hard work; and blood, sweat, tears and cash (and behaviour change). It is clearly much tougher going. And what's more, people are generally a bit too busy, a bit too tired and sometimes a bit too lazy to give that much effort. Many of them opt for the easier options requiring less effort. But from our own experience from childhood onwards, we *know* that something good won't happen without some effort.

Saving energy – the long and winding road?

Energy saving has been around since 1973 (see Figure 1.3) and surprisingly, so have mobile phones.[2] Nowadays, the mobile phone is ubiquitous, but not every organisation and its employees practise energy efficiency. Partly it was because buying energy-efficient technology seemed sufficient. Furthermore, in 1973 and the years immediately after, the aim was to save money rather than safeguard natural resources. Even in the 1990s, energy specialists in the UK were mostly technologists with very little idea of how to motivate or engage people. I recall my early days with the UK Government's Energy Efficiency Best Practice programme in the 1990s when we ran workshops telling people how to read electricity meters.[3] By outsourcing energy efficiency activities to our technical colleagues, we may have put it in an unfashionable corporate ghetto with its own particular set of incomprehensible jargon, leaving most of the organisation to believe that energy saving was the sole responsibility of the specialists, not themselves.

Despite the Triple Bottom Line making its presence in 1991, environmental management went much the same way in the mid-1990s with a lot of technology and even more monitoring. The volume of environmental legislation put an impersonal distance between the topic and the average worker. When sustainability came into vogue, its diversity managed to include more people, but it was also stuck with a green label, which put off some other people.

In contrast, the mobile phone hid much of the technology from the users and extolled the benefits, which are highly visible. Consequently, we see little problem with paying a monthly fee and upgrading every few years. The mobile phone people got the marketing right – happy people living great lives having fun with their phones. Sustainability is still about lots of monitoring and getting hectored about not printing your emails or switching off lights. It's not surprising that there seemed to be no light at the end of the energy-efficient tunnel.

However, Everyday Sustainability covers a very wide range of corporate activities and provides financial gains, customer satisfaction, staff motivation and growth and process improvement. The activities to deliver these benefits are also part of corporate good practice. The outcomes mentioned above are actually what all successful organisations are aiming for. Figure 9.1 shows how these are linked with good business practice (and common sense), and world-class

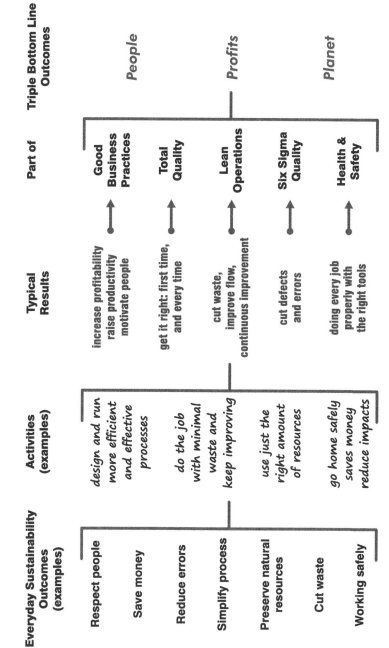

Figure 9.1 Everyday Sustainability and the Triple Bottom Line.

techniques such as Lean and Six Sigma can all be delivered through Everyday Sustainability. Furthermore, all these activities come under the umbrella of the Triple Bottom Line: effective management of people, profit and planet.

Since this is all good stuff, and we already know that doing good stuff means putting in some effort, we just need to get the idea through to our busy, tired or lazy colleagues.

So we come to marketing and communications and perhaps to the accompanying smoke and mirrors, as well as the hype? Not true at all; we know we've got a good thing in doing Everyday Sustainability, since it is good for our organisation, for us as people and, through our actions, for the world as a whole. We do not need smoke, mirrors or hype to help us. What we do need is a message that captures our colleagues' attention as well as communications to keep their attention for a little while thereafter. We also need senior management's buy-in to get it started and to keep up the momentum.

Getting senior management to buy into your proposal needs a string of persuasive arguments, and once you've got your facts covered with plenty of relevant evidence, you can readily go through a cascade of arguments (well, perhaps reasons) as shown in Figure 9.2. You will need a range of persuasive messages because your target audiences may respond to one particular argument but perhaps not to others. Some of this was covered in Chapter 8 about developing a series of answers when proposing an Everyday Sustainability initiative to the boss.

The contents of your message are, however, much more straightforward. I recommend you stick to the easy, simple and practical approach. Mainly because senior people are not necessarily familiar with the minutiae of daily activities at the working level, and you want to keep it easy to understand and avoid jargon. You also need to keep it simple because these people are busy and don't have time for a lot of fuzzy and convoluted statements. Practical, because senior people are often practical people; something that is altogether too esoteric may not get you very far. However, senior people are still people and most have some idealism about doing sustainability, or at least, the sense to be seen to care about sustainability, and you should appeal to that sentiment.

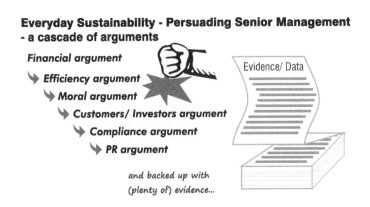

Figure 9.2 Everyday Sustainability – Persuading Senior Management.

We therefore come to the point about active persuasion and perhaps deploying some specific techniques here can help. The Internet has lots web pages on "rules of persuasion;"[4] these range from the Robert Cialdini's Six Principles[5] to Forbes magazine's 21 principles.[6] Essentially persuasion is the gift wrapping on your Everyday Sustainability idea.

Basically all these various techniques to persuade people contain similar suggestions only phrased differently and packaged very differently (and some are quite long-winded). They also go on about being ethical in using these rules but let's have a reality check: these are the same techniques used by fraudsters, grifters and con-men because they actually work!

For brevity, I will describe Robert Cialdini's Six Principles and show how they can be used to promote Everyday Sustainability. Cialdini, a persuasion/influence expert, starts with saying that people only get persuaded if they wanted to be persuaded, so you cannot change people's behaviour if your target is disinclined. Your proposal, therefore, needs to hit the logical, emotional and personal targets of your audience. His six principles of persuasion are summarised in Table 9.2.

Combining these six principles with some marketing techniques such as the 4P Marketing Mix,[7] described below, and you are then on your way towards building an effective packaging for your Everyday Sustainability proposal, as shown in Figure 9.3.

Table 9.2 Cialdini's Six Principles of Persuasion

Reciprocation	Returning favours is part of human nature, and reciprocation of the staff's efforts in Everyday Sustainability can range from recognition to Gain Share rewards.
Commitment & consistency	If we develop a personal commitment to a concept, idea or an initiative, such as Everyday Sustainability, we are more likely to remain consistent in our adoption. For example, having ownership of the improvement ideas and being recognised for it can help in developing commitment and subsequent consistency in deploying and using the improvement.
Social proof	If all our competitors are doing sustainability and our customers are requesting it, then we cannot afford to miss out. Or if most parts of the organisation have bought into Everyday Sustainability, then there is likely to be a groundswell for the remaining ones to join in as well.
Liking	If we present a non-threatening and supportive approach to propose or promote Everyday Sustainability, and fronted by a well-liked person, then it is more likely to be easier to get buy-in.
Authority	If we appear sincere and communicate to our audience with integrity and in the right context, as well as not being overly idealistic or unrealistic, then people are more likely to believe us.
Scarcity	If Everyday Sustainability is presented as a unique opportunity for the staff to come up with ideas and be rewarded, then people will value it more (at least initially until it becomes a part of your corporate culture).

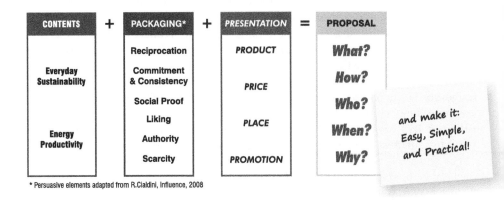

* Persuasive elements adapted from R.Cialdini, Influence, 2008

Figure 9.3 From Concept to Action – Contents, Packaging, Presentation and Proposal.

The components of Figure 9.3 deal with various requirements: the contents offer the details, the marketing (or the packaging) aims to persuade and the presentation deals with the pragmatic and logistical issues. The proposal puts these together in a structured and easy to understand format: the actions required and the benefits.

Uncertainty often means people want to find out more.[8] The message communicated in your proposal, therefore, needs to be precise, concise as well as simple, easy and practical. The Marketing Mix is a useful way to explore how the message can be communicated while incorporating Cialdini's principles. Your simple, easy and practical message is therefore Doing More with Less too!

The contents of your proposal should follow an initial discussion to establish the idea of the improvement project and gain approval to present a proposal. The proposal needs to include details about the improvement programme, the needs and our capabilities to deliver, the costs, timetable and what needs to be done. This area also includes the methods and the monitoring as well as the support activities, such as communications and training. If capital investments are needed, then a business case needs to be presented in the required corporate format.

The packaging includes the persuasive or marketing elements; how you transform "mere interest" to a "demand for action." You can readily combine Cialdini's six persuasive elements into your pitch, for example:

> "… *all the leading companies are doing sustainability, but we can leapfrog them with Everyday Sustainability…*" – social proof and scarcity, respectively

> "… *all the leading companies are doing sustainability, but we can leapfrog them with Everyday Sustainability. I got all these useful hints from Uly Ma's new book…*" – social proof, scarcity and authority, respectively

"*… remember our mission statement about sustainability? Well, all the leading companies are doing it, but we can leapfrog them. I got the idea of Everyday Sustainability from Uly Ma's new book…*" – commitment and consistency, social proof, scarcity and authority, respectively

(Editor: "Uly, this is a bit too blatant."

Uly: "Okay boss; all of the above are true, but maybe skip the bits promoting this book then…")

The contents and packaging make up the bulk of the proposal, but you also need to have a quick presentation of the important details ready. The 4P Marketing Mix (Figure 9.4) is a convenient technique to package the information in an easy, simple and practical format, and in many ways, it acts as the FAQ[9] for your proposal.

Marketing Mix

Product describes what is presented, ideally in one simple sentence. It needs to unambiguous and clearly structured. It is a description that says "this is what we want to do" whether it is a product, service or value-enabling activity.

Price describes all the associated costs of the initiative. Capital costs and running costs are the obvious candidates, but it should also include the associated and intangible costs. Associated costs can include the cost of communications as well as training, while the intangible costs are the Switching Costs of changing from one set of operations and behaviours to another set. This is a critical cost, as the Switching Costs[10] are often the ones that determine the

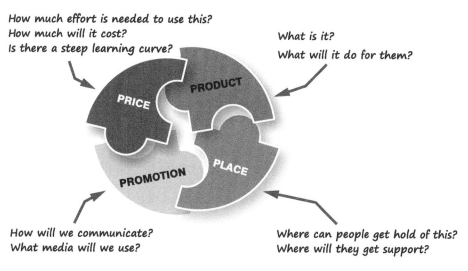

How much effort is needed to use this?
How much will it cost?
Is there a steep learning curve?

What is it?
What will it do for them?

How will we communicate?
What media will we use?

Where can people get hold of this?
Where will they get support?

Figure 9.4 The 4P Marketing Mix in Communications Planning.

success of an initiative. Addressing these costs are part of the easy/simple/practical aspects of the design, as well as staff engagement during the design stages.

It is also crucial to outline the financial benefits from the initiative to show how these estimated gains offset the envisaged costs. Do make sure, however, you are using a financial returns assessment method that is consistent with the way the organisation assesses return on investment, otherwise, you will be laughed out of the room by your finance colleagues.

Place is about where (and when) the proposed activities will take place, as well as how people can access your offerings – i.e. the logistics and distribution of whatever you are proposing. This is important, as people will need to schedule the activities into their schedules. While it is not always possible to give precise details about where and when, a general idea can be offered, for example: *"… in August this year, at our main office location and via our corporate website…"* There should also be some consideration about logistics and distribution elements of the initiative.

Promotion is about how you will communicate the details of the proposed activities to your colleagues and other relevant Stakeholders such as suppliers or customers. This means a communications plan, a reporting schedule, perhaps a support programme as well as a series of necessary briefings. On the marketing side, you may need to decide whether the proposed activities will have a specific name and unique logo, what theme to use and whether the message needs to be tailored to the various Stakeholders.

Once these details have been finalised, you will be able to answer the 5 Questions Cluster easily:

- What are we going to do?
- How will we do that?
- Who will help us?
- When do we start?
- Why are we doing this?

Answering these questions helps form the framework of your proposal and also provides much of the details.

In Chapter 7, the description of the 5 Questions Cluster shows how a set of factual information can make up a simple project plan. Although this satisfies the logical elements of decision making, it does not necessarily deal with the personal and emotional elements particularly well. However, these areas can still be supported by the persuasive packaging with specifically posed questions, as shown in Figure 9.5.

Appealing to the head through logic is about that which makes sense. This is likely to be an official endeavour, and therefore questions are about practical items in a to-do list. As it is likely to be something to do with work, the easy, simple and practical aspects matter quite a bit, since we are likely to be rushed and under-resourced.

When we are **appealing to the heart** or emotions about doing Everyday Sustainability, we are talking about doing the right thing. Most people will

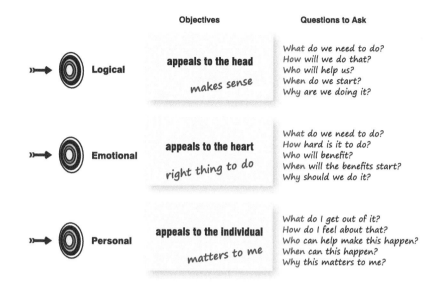

Objectives	Questions to Ask
Logical **appeals to the head** *makes sense*	What do we need to do? How will we do that? Who will help us? When do we start? Why are we doing it?
Emotional **appeals to the heart** *right thing to do*	What do we need to do? How hard is it to do? Who will benefit? When will the benefits start? Why should we do it?
Personal **appeals to the individual** *matters to me*	What do I get out of it? How do I feel about that? Who can help make this happen? When can this happen? Why this matters to me?

Figure 9.5 Hitting the Targets.

offer you an opportunity to present your ideas. Don't forget, it is generally politically correct for most people to be seen to be supporting sustainability, so this is often like pushing on a half-opened door; you just need to take into account the ego of the people you are dealing with.

Appealing to the individual colleague brings things to a personal level: what matters to an individual, here, and now. This is a different set of appeals in that people are prepared to put in a bit more effort if the rewards are desirable and personal. Simple, easy and practical become secondary to the size and impact of the reward for the individual. In many ways, this is a bit more subtle and perhaps manipulative, you need to find out what rings the individual's bell and focus your proposal accordingly. What you may need to watch out for is that if the target, say a senior manager, is not familiar with the proposed ideas, is not motivated or dislikes you, then emotional and personal aspects of the packaging can misdirect the thinking and therefore steer away from the logical aspect of the proposal. In the case of being disliked, I suggest you consider finding someone else who is more favourable than you to present the proposal.

Stakeholders

You can divide the Stakeholders in your organisation into three categories as shown in Figure 9.6.[11] They are the committed Stakeholders, involved Stakeholders and interested Stakeholders. While some of these groups can overlap, they can also be distinct from each other in terms of their relationships with you as well as your obligations to them.

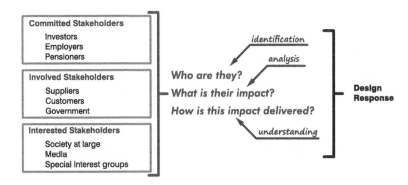

Figure 9.6 Stakeholders – The Social Aspects of Sustainability.

Committed Stakeholders generally have two main groups: investors/shareholders and employees. They are committed because they are tied to your organisation in a unique way. Investors make your organisation possible through their investments, and employees make your outputs possible through their efforts. A possible third group is made up of pensioners, as their pensions are paid by the organisation, but often their roles are similar to the interested Stakeholders described below. Activist managers of pension funds, however, have somewhat different objectives (e.g. bonus payments) and often behave in similar ways to activist shareholders.

The motivations of these groups, however, can vary somewhat when it comes to sustainability. Although both employees and investors are unlikely to desire a destruction of the global eco-system, investors and pension funds may accept sustainability actions that still offer a good return on investment, whereas workers are unlikely to welcome sustainability actions that price them out of a job. Individual pensioners tend to want their pensions paid and are somewhat more averse to corporate adventures.

Involved Stakeholders are people or organisations that have a formalised relationship with you: suppliers and customers, as well as governments. Suppliers are linked to you by legally binding contracts and customers through the functionality provided by your services or products and their respective warranties. Government has three main roles: law making, law enforcing and as a sugar daddy. The first two are self-explanatory – you break the laws they make, they will come and get you – whether tax evasion or pollution.

The government as a sugar daddy is rather different. Here, the government is supporting its businesses and service provider in the name of the greater good. Nevertheless, this was not a given historically. For example, until the Great Depression of the early 20th century, governments in general had a low level of responsibility towards unemployment. Nowadays, government support can include tax breaks, grants, loans and trade barriers. Nationalisation is an extreme example of sugar daddy action: bailing out weak or failing companies, or stealing successful ones, for the government's cronies to turn into failing companies. Often an outcome in such circumstances is some degree of government management or ownership control. However, in less extreme cases, the giving of grants, loans or tax incentives are also ways where weaker or small companies can be given a step up towards a more competitive future.

Sustainability has often benefited from such government largess; incentives towards energy efficiency investments, for example, are popular. Nevertheless, there really is no such thing as a free lunch, and someone, usually the taxpayer, pays for these incentives. Nonetheless, there is no reason not to hold your hand out to your government to get some support for your Everyday Sustainability initiative – grants, loans and publicity. By tying your Everyday Sustainability initiative to a government strategy (whether national, regional or local – there is always some sustainability or productivity initiatives going on), you can even do them a favour by showing: (1) how enthusiastic your support is and (2) how their support (grants etc.) resulted in your success.

The interested Stakeholders are probably the most diverse group of Stakeholders. They have no legal or contractual links with your organisation other than sharing the same address – the Earth. These can include neighbours, the media, fellow citizens and passionate believers of various political/social/ ecological persuasion. Their roles can include interested observers, watchdogs, supporters, protesters, inconvenienced citizens, reporters and saboteurs. With social media, their voices can be heard and their opinions, whether based on facts or fiction, can be very influential.

In an uncertain word of "fake news," the impact of these groups can be quite substantial, and the problem is that there is no easy way of satisfying everyone. A disgruntled employee can find support through the Internet for virtually any claim, and perhaps resulting in fake news that damages the organisation. Similarly, an unhappy investor can gather support through the media to try to reverse a corporate decision.

Dealing with the diverse groups of Stakeholders requires a range of policies and actions in the right context. My suggestions are either to treat these groups and their interactions with you as risk issues or problems. You can then use the FMEA or DMAIC techniques to address them in a comprehensive and systematic way. By the way, this is not conventional Stakeholder management but instead a somewhat paranoid/pessimistic approach. But if you are exploring known and unknown risks, then it may be better to be prepared than to be nice.

Remember, individually your investors, employees, suppliers and government can all be your customers too. Mass market products such as banking services, entertainment, food and drink, pharmaceutical and transport are, for example, sectors that have all these three Stakeholder groups as customers, and the relation between these Stakeholders and the organisation is therefore more complex and multi-faceted.

This brings us to the next chapter, exploring what is needed to keep a strategy on track.

Notes

1 Remember the Brexit leavers' claim that the UK will save £350 million a week if Brexit happened? Now the EU is telling the UK that it needs to pay a €100 billion divorce settlement – probably all lies from both sides.

2 Apparently a Motorola researcher made the first call in April 1973 with a mobile phone that weighed 1.1 kg and was 23 cm long.

3 We then received complaints that since the meters we brought to the workshops were not the same as the ones the audience had in their workplace, it was therefore not useful to them ....

4 Google returned 15 million plus hits on "rules of persuasion" when I checked in July 2016.

5 Cialdini has an insightful and fun video, the Science of Persuasion, on these Six Principles available on You Tube. He has also written lots of books on the subject of influence, including a comic!

6 Check it out at the *Forbes* website; the 21 rules were first launched in 2013.

7 In Chapter 7 and Figure 7.6, the Marketing Mix was used as parameters in a Criticality Assessment. Here it is used as a part of a marketing and communications strategy – its original role.

8 When British Airways suffered a major IT failure in May 2017 and cancelled all their flights globally, a major complaint (among many) is: "nobody tells us what is happening".

9 Frequently Asked Questions – a favourite on many websites that usually misses *your* particular question!

10 See Chapter 7, Figure 7.14 and Appendix 2 for more details.

11 Also described in Chapter 3 and Figure 3.5.

10 Keeping it going

What is a good antidote for uncertainty? I would argue that it is having suffi-cient resources to protect yourself against any fallout and being ready to take advantage of any opportunity. In this book, I introduced Everyday Sustain-ability as such an antidote for uncertainty. We have explored auditing your organisation to find out what is going on, spotting and dealing with problems through reducing waste – to Do More with Less – and finally to establish an initiative to make this happen. So far, we have covered most of the necessary building blocks, and this chapter concludes the book by exploring the last few essential elements of Everyday Sustainability.

Keeping the Everyday Sustainability initiative going is not just about the improvement programme activities described in Chapter 7 or a coherent and consistent strategy, but also the ancillary and supporting actions that enable it to become a part of the organisation's culture. These are shown in Figure 10.1. This chapter reviews these actions and outlines some quick wins as well as pitfalls to avoid.

Figure 10.1 Enabling a Lasting Everyday Sustainability Initiative.

The Supporting Acts

Equipment upgrade

This may seem a very strange way to motivate people, but surprisingly it works. I remember one of my early bosses who, upon hearing of our successful metallurgy research project, suggested that we now had approval for a new microscope.[1] This motivated my team, as they felt more valued (needless to say, we ordered the most expensive top-end model, knowing that further upgrades were unlikely to come again in our lifetime). Anecdotes aside, an equipment upgrade can often make work much easier. Furthermore, even a furniture upgrade can boost morale. However, this can also go badly wrong if an organisation goes about it in an idiosyncratic way. A colleague at a public transport company told me that their employer offered to modernise their office. That was well received until they saw the walls ended up greyish magnolia (a shade of paint only corporate bureaucrats can find), the posters turned out to be corporate promotional posters and the plants, well, they were plastic! You can imagine what that did for morale.

Support

Not everyone will need support, and, more importantly, not everyone will know that they need support. Support includes letting people know there is no shame in asking for help and also that help is available without criticism or admonishment (within reason). Support is also about identifying people who are having difficulties and/or are too proud or shy to say so.

People also have other reasons to need support, and Figure 10.2 shows some of the underlying issues people may be facing and perhaps not too keen to say out loud. Nonetheless, they all need support of one kind or another to ensure that your Everyday Sustainability programme goes well.

Is there a universal formula for dealing with this? But what is "support?" Is it a shoulder to cry on? Targeted training? Discounted gym membership? Or is it a coach who helps you find yourself? Support can be any or all of these things. The main thing is to make sure people know that someone will listen to them and also be willing to provide extra explanations, some training and perhaps cut them a bit of slack. Of course, you are usually pushed for time, but spending a little time sorting something out before the problem gets big is always a better investment than sorting it out when the whole thing blows up.[2]

What is needed besides listening? Having a support framework built into an improvement project is a worthwhile investment. The Gains from the improvement, if realised successfully, will readily repay the investment. The support framework can be linked to both the training programme as well as the project communications. In addition, the project team members, facilitators and trainers will also need training on how to spot people who need help.

Figure 10.2 Different Needs ... Different Support.

Training

As your processes, procedures and culture evolve and change, your staff needs to be up-to-date on both the associated technical aspects and the behavioural, communications and relationship aspects. You therefore need to explore ways of getting your people to become knowledge workers.[3] I would suggest you consider knowledge workers not just as people who "think for a living," like architects, engineers, scientists, accountants, lawyers and so on, but also any worker who can analyse a situation critically to solve problems: including hairdressers, construction workers, chefs and many others who spend a significant portion of their days solving problems.

Before you complain that "we don't want these people to think," you need to consider that these people are more likely to have a better understanding of what they are doing than you, since they do it every day. They may not be as well educated as many managers, but in my experience, people doing the job usually have easy, simple and practical ideas of how to do them better, and I believe that most people do want to make things better. However, it is sometimes scary to raise your hand in front of your colleagues and suggest, "We can do better than this." This difficulty comes sometimes from a lack of confidence but more often from incomplete knowledge and a lack of effective communications skills, as highlighted in Figure 10.3. Not being able to overcome these barriers can mean your organisation loses out on new ideas and innovations (which I will explore later in this chapter).

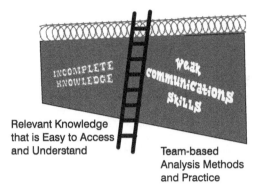

Figure 10.3 Overcoming Barriers.

If you want ideas from your people to help you improve your Everyday Sustainability performance, you need to make it easy for them to contribute. From this position, these barriers are not hard to overcome, and a small investment in time and effort to make sure people have sufficient skills to present their ideas can only benefit everybody. Letting people have sufficient information and knowledge so that they can make useful decisions and contributions is a no-brainer. Enabling people to do this will raise morale as well as contribute towards a rising Energy Productivity Key Performance Indicator (KPI).

Innovation

Everyday Sustainability is based on people taking care about what they do and then looking for ways to do better or to innovate. By adopting this approach of continuous improvement, the organisation's Energy Productivity KPI can start going up.

Nevertheless, innovation is an area that has always bothered organisations: just about every organisation wants it, but not everyone knows how to get there. Companies like 3M and Google seem to innovate with ease, but can we copy their strategies of allocating 15 hours each month for every staff member to innovate? Anyway, what is an innovation? Is it reinventing the wheel? Or is it about developing a better mousetrap? I think we need to differentiate between invention and innovation. To make our lives easier, I suggest the following pragmatic definitions:

- Invention is about something new or rolling back the frontiers of knowledge. Value is uncertain at this point, as nobody knows what benefits it will bring to the world.
- Innovation is something "better" or refining what is already known to improve effectiveness, efficiency or value. So it is about doing things differently or doing different things to achieve the same goal.

For most organisations, Everyday Sustainability is about innovation, and this itself can be divided into two sub-categories: disruptive innovation and sustaining innovation. A disruptive innovation upsets the established rules with new rules, whereas a sustaining innovation extends the established rules and maintains the "trend." Most incremental improvements are sustaining innovations. Figure 10.4 shows an example of this through several generations of data storage, both sustaining and disruptive.

Another good example of the two types of innovation is the Uber taxi app vs. traditional taxis. Uber threatened the traditional model of taxi service with its innovative approach to pricing, but this spurred traditional taxis to respond more flexibly. For example, London's black cabs now offer fixed fare for some routes as well as discounts for longer journeys.

You need to have certain enabling conditions in place to get an innovative atmosphere going in your organisation, as shown in Figure 10.5. There must be a corporate willingness to encourage innovations as well as an open attitude to accept changes. These policies need to be accompanied with the right tools and skills together with individuals who are willing to explore and persevere with their initiatives. Finally, there should be a need for change – whether at the organisational level or at the local level – if people cannot see a need for change, then any tinkering with processes and procedures can become something for personal satisfaction.

For an individual, change activities are often self-directed and focussed mainly on oneself or one's nearest circle. However, in a team, the changes brought about by innovation are usually adopted by consensus, which requires an extra degree of organisation and formality. In a corporate environment, the strategic direction for innovation needs to be (and usually is) top down, and this often comes with a more detailed framework and (alas) more rules.

Nonetheless, the actual path of an Everyday Sustainability innovation is actually quite straightforward. It is made up of four stages: coming up with

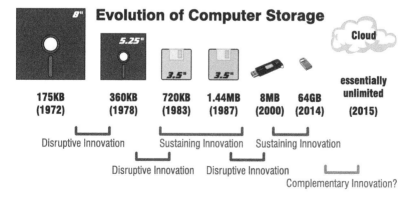

Figure 10.4 Sustaining and Disruptive Innovation Example – Evolution of Computer Storage.

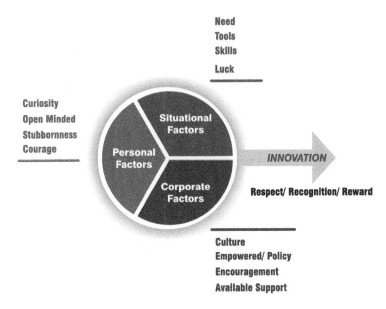

Figure 10.5 Enabling Innovation.

the innovation, spreading the word to a few colleagues, time passing and general adoption taking place. Let's look at these in some more detail, as shown in Figure 10.6.

Coming up with the innovation

This requires an individual (or several individuals) to be willing to suggest that things can be done better. The next step can either be intuitive: a "eureka" moment like Archimedes in the bath, or something more systematic: where the "this can be done better" is treated as a problem that needs a solution and dealt with accordingly.

Can you recruit these people or can your nurture your existing colleagues? My feelings are that if people are not afraid, then they are more likely to speak out. If the corporate culture allows it, then speaking out can lead to doing something about it. If all these are set in a framework with some degree of corporate openness and support, then bit-by-bit people will come forward with ideas. This can be reinforced with an appropriate recognition and rewards scheme (explored later in this chapter). If, however, the culture is one where the managers and leaders claim all the credit for the successful ideas, then the well will definitely go dry very quickly.

Dissemination – stage 1

The initial communications are usually through networking: people who share an interest and are also keen to try out the idea. The communications

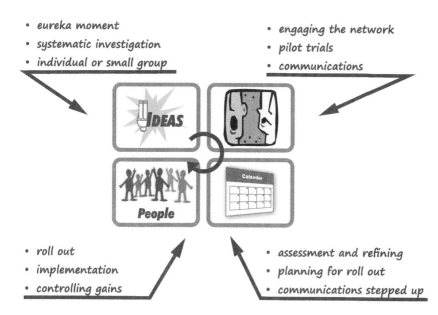

Figure 10.6 Innovation Timeline – from Idea to Roll Out.

strategy at this stage is generally fairly easy, as the message is homogeneous. For example, geeks share the concept via their own jargon, and the information passes quickly to the other individuals. Furthermore, the individuals in this group tend to respect the original innovator who is one of them. These synergies make dissemination and adoption much easier.

The initial network group members can act as champions and promote the ideas to other groups and networks. While this is good for spreading the idea, some colleagues may find the excessive zeal overwhelming (especially if spiced with jargon) or even threatening.

In a more formal environment, the organisation may establish pilot trials and tests to explore the full possible values from the innovation, as well as releasing information through its formal communications channels. Senior managers may be advised of the innovation informally at this stage, with greater or lesser details depending on the propensity of the management team to help or meddle.

In the case of Everyday Sustainability, success usually means waste reduction and, with it, cost reduction. Therefore the communications message can be quite positive and directly motivating to the network and to any managers involved.

Time passes

The initial ideas and activities are often accompanied with trials and redevelopments where minor problems and teething issues are resolved. The network is kept informed, and they further spread the message to additional networks.

The corporate communications framework may release more information, and the organisation may start to review plans for a larger rollout for the training and support system required. This is the time to put a corporate programme with detailed policy statements, communication themes, activities and targets for Everyday Sustainability initiative into action.

The innovator may also collect enthusiastic colleagues and establish informal teams to further refine the original innovation.

This kind of thing tends to happen faster in more progressive organisations, but for the rest of us, it can be plain hard work trying to spread the word and looking for champions.

Dissemination – stage 2

Times passes, and the ideas percolate through to the broader audience, and the communications model starts to change from predominantly networking to more and more marketing. The message needs to take into account the profile of the broader audience as well as the culture of the various audience segments. The early majority of adopters is a larger audience than the initial networking group, and therefore the message for them will need to be more general in nature and with less jargon. The refined innovation may be rolled out to the entire organisation at this stage with accompanying communications, training and support frameworks.

Targets are identified and agreed on, and the implementation teams are trained and ready to start. This is when the corporate Everyday Sustainability initiative kicks into high gear.

At this stage, the later adopters may still be sceptical, but the corporate momentum may be driving them towards deploying the innovation. They are also likely to require a greater degree of support and communications to overcome any doubts, scepticism and concerns.

What about the laggards – the people who do not welcome changes or innovations?

Unfortunately, these people do exist in every organisation, and they are just like you and me, except they do not like to be part of this endeavour. The reactions from the change resistors can range from apathy all the way to total disengagement and active sabotage. The best-case scenario is that they will leave the organisation and the worst case is probably active sabotage of the innovation. In between is a range of reactions, from apathy to mild resistance. If you have decided that these people cannot be persuaded to become supporters, then you need to persuade them towards minimal engagement with the programme. You also need to identify and isolate those who are not going to change their behaviour. Then put in place procedures that will minimise or isolate any negative impact.

Before going to this point, it is worthwhile to find out why people are unhappy about change. This brings on a question: Since Everyday Sustainability has virtually no downsides, then why are people not engaging? We adopted the Easy–Simple–Practical approach and we have developed straightforward ways to tackle problems, what is left? There is always the "not invented here" reason, the "not interested" reason, the "nothing in it for me" reason and the "don't understand" reason, but these can often be attributed to the organisation not showing sufficient appreciation. The next section explores showing appreciation in three ways: respect, recognition and rewards.

The 3Rs

Showing appreciation for its workers is often a concern for some organisations, and the reasons generally include "we can't afford it." This is a common theme from profit-sharing programmes where a reduction in the sharing can result in a major plunge in morale. But showing appreciation does not need be expensive; in fact, we can easily Do More with Less in this area. I suggest organisations take a three-pronged approach in showing appreciation, as described in Figure 10.7: Respect, Recognition and Rewards, or the 3Rs.[4]

Respect is very simple but has a tremendous impact. If your organisation does not respect its individual employees (or contractors), then why select them to become staff members in the first place? Many employers often demonstrate a significant lack of respect for their front-line or lower-level

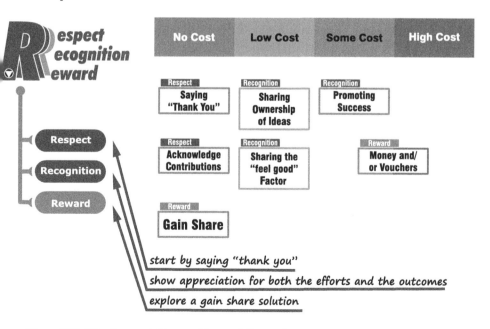

Figure 10.7 3Rs: Respect, Recognition and Reward.

staff, and since people usually respond in kind, then an atmosphere of mutual disrespect can affect the outcomes of corporate initiatives. Respect is also the starting point of building trust and partnership in an organisation, and for Everyday Sustainability to work you will need both.

Respecting all your colleagues also means respecting their efforts to innovate and solve problems where they work, even if their efforts do not bear fruit immediately. Generally, people doing the job often have the most relevant ideas for solving the problem, and they are more likely to stick at it until it works as intended.

So how do you start with respect? Saying thank you is a very simple and easy starting point (and even better if you actually look at the person you are saying thanks to). Then there is listening. Everyone has views and ideas to express, but we are often so busy that we do not find the time to listen, especially if our colleague is less than eloquent. Showing respect means acknowledging the contributions by everyone, especially colleagues who are perhaps a bit shy, more junior in rank or less gifted in their presentation. Then you will be on the path to build trust and partnership in your organisation.

Recognising both the effort and the outcomes are important, but are they equally important? I think effort needs to be recognised but perhaps not to the same degree as achievement. You want to encourage experimentation in terms of innovations, but you do not want to encourage serial failures. This is where support for the innovations comes in, and people who are trying to reinvent the square wheel need to be put onto a different path rather than going nowhere over and over.

Achievements and outcomes are different than effort: they signify success, and therefore recognition is the right response. Can we show recognition besides giving a bonus? Of course. We can share the ownership of the idea with the individual or the team by letting the whole organisation know that our colleagues came up with the idea that raised the Energy Productivity last month, for example. We can further promote their great ideas to the outside world through case studies or items placed in news blogs/media. Through these various channels, we are telling the world that our colleagues are special. Besides these, recognition can also come from winning in-house awards.

And then there are the **Rewards** we can offer: money, gift vouchers or other incentives such as a paid trip to a popular musical. But the memory of the rewards can slip as fast as the money/gifts/incentives are spent or used. A big problem with rewards based on money is that after a while people start to treat them as a regular part of the salary or wages (whether anything is achieved or not), and this can create a sense of entitlement.

Can rewards happen without money of some sort? Yes, up to a point. Eventually, for any initiative to be sustainable, some long-term rewards need to be in place, and probably the best way to go forward for Everyday Sustainability is Gain Share.

Gain Share

Gain Share came out of the Scanlon Plan[5] where Gains from savings were shared in an open and agreed way between the company and the employees. This is not profit sharing, as the money comes from savings – money that was lost in the organisation through inefficiency, ineffectiveness and waste. This immediately gets rid of the "we can't afford it" argument often heard from management.

Since the Gains come from waste reduction, then everyone benefits in a number of ways including: safe-guarding jobs, a more pleasant workplace, more respect and trust as well as more MONEY!

Traditional Gain Share splits this between the organisation and the employees through various simple and complex formulae. The constant element is an openness about the Gains and sticking to the previously agreed distribution of the Gains. Generally, a traditional model would split the Gains two ways: adding to the profits or cash-in-hand for the organisation and sharing the rest with every member of the staff. There may be some scheduling finesse in working out when the sharing takes place.

For Everyday Sustainability, I would like to propose a different Gain Share model, as shown in Figure 10.8. In addition to the two elements described above, some of the Gains should go to the teams that come up with the innovations; some of the Gains should go towards strategic corporate goals like apprenticeships/internships, extra vocational training; and finally, a meaningful proportion should go to one or more local partners such as schools, charities or social enterprises. This brings the organisation and community closer together and doesn't just generate good will, but also adds value to society. Does doing social good benefit the organisation? Perhaps not immediately, but it can show others your organisation's compassionate nature, which is attractive to customers. Furthermore, being active in the community can help establish a positive reputation, which may result in more successful recruitment in the future. Doing social good also makes the staff feel good, which is very important for morale and builds a progressive corporate culture. When it actually helps other people in society, it is even better, and, best of all, it actually does not cost your organisation any money since it comes from recovered waste.

I described the range of social sustainability activities organisations can explore in my book *No Waste* and how to engage the staff (both contractors and employees) in exploring the ways an organisation can support its community. Sharing the Gains with social partners can be *ad hoc*, as in a direct grant to, say, a local school or charity, it can be semi-structured as in the organisation offering staff time to physically take part in local social activities such as a neighbourhood tidying up. A more formal type of social sustainability is to support social enterprise projects that are directed to specific sections of society.

My colleague Rebecca Lovelace[6] of Circle Three Consulting offered me an example of a formal social partnership programme, BuildingPeople, which she is leading. This type of structured activities is best suited for a multi-year support from a Gain Share programme.

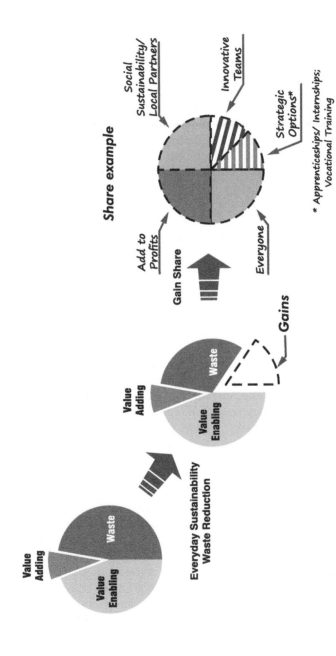

Figure 10.8 The Gain Share Process.

BuildingPeople – a social enterprise

According to Rebecca, the UK's construction industry after Brexit is expected to lose up to 176,500 foreign workers, but it will also need 179,000 additional construction workers to fill the new jobs created by 2021. The industry, however, regularly complains of skills and worker shortages and that the current systems of supply and demand appear unable to fulfil this. So there is a people gap of 350,000, which needs to be dealt with if the industry is to continue to provide decent jobs as well as 6.5 per cent of the UK's economic output.

The issue is often compounded by a mismatch of people seeking work, including diverse and disadvantaged groups – women, ex-offenders, unemployed, ex-military and youth. It is not necessarily a simple problem, as the industry is gradually becoming more skills-led, but many of these job seekers are not necessarily qualified in the right topics or at the right level.

The BuildingPeople initiative offers one way to make this easier for both job seekers and employers by developing a digital marketplace that connects workers to employers, jobseekers to mentors and provides access to targeted career information and resources. By engaging construction clients, developers, contractors and industry bodies, as well as local and central government and other interested parties, it is envisaged that employers, job seekers and the industry will all benefit from its collaborative framework, therefore allowing local planning development and business support teams to explore the skills and employee requirements for future projects, as well as enabling employers to measure and report on their social impact.

The initiative is a partnership between employers, central government, trade bodies as well as other initiatives that support career and skills development.

There is no reason why such initiatives should not become part of any organisation's Gain Share process. Not only do these activities help individuals and communities, it also helps to ensure a supply of skilled candidates and continued goodwill from society.

Working out the Gain Share formula is often a shared effort between the finance department and the HR department. Gain Share from Everyday Sustainability is simpler, however, as the Gains are based on Energy Productivity Gains and the overall Value Added. The Gain parameters can therefore be worked out quite easily for, say, each quarter and by logging the implemented innovations during the same period.

Who should run the Gain Share programme in the organisation? The mechanics should still involve the finance and HR teams, but the decision on how the Gains are to be measured needs to involve everyone as do the agreements on how the Shares are distributed.

When Gain Share goes wrong

Gain Share can take some time to plan, to work out an equitable Share out and to monitor it thereafter, but once it is set up, it is very easy to dismantle. In fact, it only takes one word: greed.

If any of the recipient parties think that their Share is not sufficient (or think that someone else's Share is too big) then Gain Share can unravel quickly – through infighting or through a refusal to participate.

The organisation may decide that it is giving too much money away to its workforce and decide to retain more of the Gains by reducing the other's Share of the Gains. Then it is likely that the stream of innovative ideas (and the stream of Gain) will dry up. There are apocryphal stories of managers resenting their workers getting an ever-increasing Gain Share payout and decided to stop or cut back (the stories are not too clear on this) the Gain Share programme, and surprise, surprise, the cost-saving ideas stopped.

Another impact to consider when Gain Share goes wrong is the Share commitments made to outside partners. Not only will there be disappointment, but also a major loss of goodwill, which may damage the organisation's reputation.

How do you safeguard against greed? A strong champion helps, but so does having a Gain Share charter and a management committee that comprises members from all branches of the organisation; strong involvement with external partners can also protect the Gain Share initiative. But perhaps most important is the organisation's culture. If the organisation sees Gain Share as an outcome from a partnership between the organisation and its employees and treats this partnership with respect, then there is a good chance that these threats may not occur.

Continuous improvement – the different roles of change agent

Everyday Sustainability is a continuous improvement activity; you are unlikely to reach perfection quickly and are therefore always improving your performance. Carrying out a continuous improvement process can be summarised by the Plan/Do/Check/Act (PDCA) Deming Cycle described in Chapter 7.

What are the various underpinning activities that allow improvements to keep the improvement culture going? One of the requirements is to have change agents. To assist you, I have compiled a set of change agent Frequently Asked Questions (with answers) below.

1   What is a change agent?

This is a special person (or persons) that helps shape opinion for change, enables changes in culture and delivers the improvement programme. In fact, a change agent has a portfolio of functions: developing a need or change, enabling information exchange, diagnosing problems, shaping behaviour, creating an organisational intent to change, turning this intent into action and sustaining this action.

A change agent does not have to be the innovator, but s/he must have a reasonably complete understanding of the innovation as well as knowing what needs to be done.

2   Can I become a change agent?

Yes, in principle, everyone can be a change agent. In reality, you will need to have some enthusiasm for the improvement or some useful skills in the implementation of the change.

3   Do I need to be a senior manager?

Ideally the change agent is someone either with sufficient authority to make change happen or has been delegated with sufficient authority to deliver change. They need to be able to bring in champions who definitely should be corporate heavyweights, as they (eventually) will need to drive through any change resistance or budget barriers to make things happen.

The champion also acts as a safety warning system for the change agent in situations where corporate decisions and directions change rapidly.

4   What about being an innovator?

I believe change agents need to be more than innovators; they need to have some project or programme management skills, as they have to take on the day-to-day activities of an improvement initiative. In fact, there is no reason why a change agent needs to be an innovator at all. Think about all the senior managers you read about who were brought in to turn a company around – they are not necessary inventors but they are often implementers.

5   What do I have to do as a change agent?

Figure 10.9 outlines the main roles a change agent needs to be able to carry out. Let's have a look at these and see how they contribute to Everyday Sustainability. I divided these into two main areas: preparing and doing.

Figure 10.9 The Various Roles of a Change Agent.

Preparing

Exploration – A change agent needs to be looking for opportunities where the improvement can benefit the largest number of people, whether staff, suppliers, customers or other Stakeholders. To do this role well, you will need access to information about the organisation and an awareness of social/cultural trends.

Analysis – What do people want? Understanding the issues that concerns the Stakeholders, whether committed (staff/investors), involved (customers/suppliers) or the interested (neighbours/society), means that the dissemination can be better tailored to ensure a greater chance of success.

Matchmaking – Which opportunity matches best with the corporate objectives? Which ones is most in tune with the times? With our society's trends? Getting this right makes take-up much easier in an organisation.

Coordinating – the skills and capabilities of project managers is a major help in the daily management of the initiative. This means planning, scheduling and budgeting knowledge at a level sufficient to oversee these areas.

Once the options have been decided, it is time for the "doing."

Doing

Marketing and Sales – this is about communicating information to a diverse audience, ranging from the enthusiasts to the apathetic. It also means some idea of how to influence decision making through presenting the information in a relevant way.

Cheerleading – This is about enthusiasm (and how to fake it on occasions if necessary!). The role here is to be relentlessly enthusiastic about the initiative such that it diffuses through to the other people around you. However, some judgement is also needed; being enthusiastic is not the same as preaching. Sustainability has always had a "green aura," which can annoy some people when the enthusiasm goes overboard to proselytising. You want to get people involved – turn them on rather than turn them off.

Leading – this is the role in leading projects and programmes through personality (charisma), knowledge (specialist knowledge), position (corporate ranking) and drive (getting it done).

6   Wow, lots of roles – I think I'll let someone else be the change agent, what do you think?

When recruiting a change agent, you can go for someone who is an enthusiastic staff member with specific knowledge of the organisation, or you can go for a professional change agent. These people will not know too much about the fine details of your organisation, but they know change management and what will work and what won't. The professional change agent brings experiences from other organisations, as well as new ideas of how to go about running improvement initiatives.

If budgets allow, then a partnering of a professional change agent with an in-house enthusiast will allow transferring of knowledge and skills to the organisation as well as making sure that the improvement campaign stays on track.

Supply chain and customers

Everyday Sustainability is an approach that can be brought to suppliers and communicated to customers and other Stakeholders.

Everyday Sustainability in the supply chain is not just about cost savings via enhanced logistics or reducing the carbon footprint, but also about reputation (yours) and social kudos points (shared with your Stakeholders). Through Everyday Sustainability, you can help your supplier reduce its costs and also engage its workforce. This is especially crucial in many contracted-out services such as facilities management. Lower cost is all very well, but it is how these costs are achieved that is important. A supplier who exploits its workforce to give you a lower cost can be disastrous for your reputation if something goes wrong. Similarly, a supplier with poor governance is also a potential source of embarrassment. The preference of contracting-out services nowadays means that serious attention is needed to bring all these different supplier teams together in a partnership with a shared aim of delivering value to the end user.

You can check a supplier's Energy Productivity figures over a period of time to see whether it is a well-run company and whether its values and effectiveness are in line with your expectations. It should not be a sole criterion for selecting a supplier but it can certainly be a useful parameter among many used in the selection process.

Nonetheless, with Energy Productivity being a new thing, it is unlikely that many in your supply chain will have ready figures to hand. So why not introduce them to this KPI?

Customers can be made aware of your Everyday Sustainability progress through newsletter outreach campaigns, case studies and open days. There you can showcase your ever-improving Energy Productivity KPI with the projects that made it so. This can improve the profile of your organisation and assure them that they are dealing with an organisation that operates effectively, efficiently and with integrity.

Internal and external marketing/communications

Marketing can be simplified to encourage people to make a positive decision towards you. Seen in this light, we realise that we have been doing various marketing acts since we were old enough to wheedle some goodies from our parents.

In promoting and communicating Everyday Sustainability, we have two audiences: the internal audience within the organisation and the external audience outside the gates. Now, these two groups also overlap with various

Stakeholder segments, and this makes marketing and communications more difficult. I start with looking at the differences described in Figure 10.10.

The internal audience is generally the more difficult group to convince, since they observe the daily behaviour of the decision makers or senior leaders and draw conclusions often based on what they see and not what is said. This means the internal audience can be more cynical and also more critical. Marketing and communications with this group perhaps needs to be more honest and pragmatic, for example: "... yes, social sustainability is all very well, but if we are not turning a profit, we may not be able to afford it..."

If there is one thing most employees will support, it is job security, and Everyday Sustainability is one path towards achieving that. Employees will readily consider particular options if they see these as a way to preserve (their) jobs. For example, it was reported[7] that at Galeries Lafayette, a major department store in Paris, 92 per cent of staff voted in favour of Sunday trading and 62 per cent voted to work extra hours in response to a fear of losing trade. At a time of uncertainty, honesty is likely to be a good way to convince your internal audience, especially if the leaders demonstrate their intent through their own behaviour.

An external audience, including customers, investors, society and government, is somewhat different; they generally have less information unless there are whistle blowers or indiscrete social media messages about. Therefore, active persuasion through the perceived value of the products and services, as well as the social responsibility of the organisation, are likely to be the main

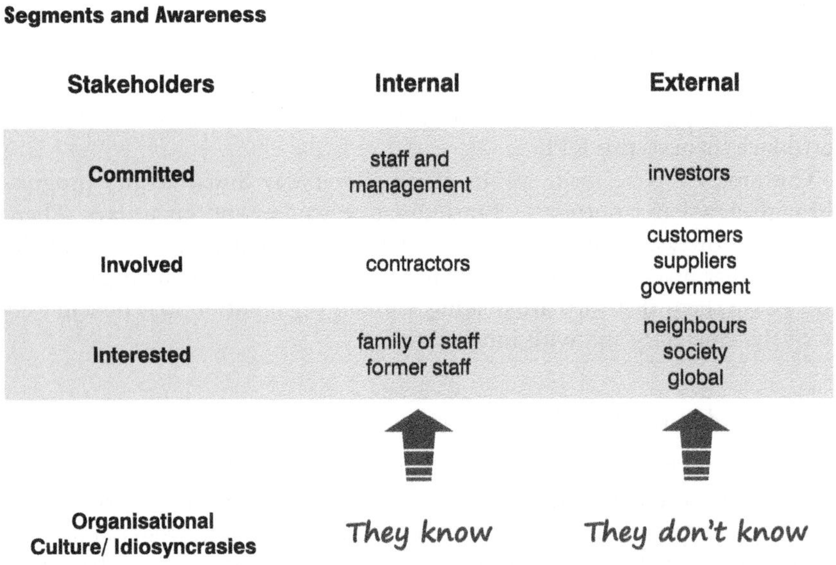

Segments and Awareness

Stakeholders	Internal	External
Committed	staff and management	investors
Involved	contractors	customers suppliers government
Interested	family of staff former staff	neighbours society global
Organisational Culture/ Idiosyncrasies	*They know*	*They don't know*

Figure 10.10 Internal and External Communications and Marketing.

thrusts to attract and retain the external audience. Stories about the staff achieving Everyday Sustainability, suitably promoted, can also provide some added value to excite the external audience. Success stories can also motivate the internal audience, and if you are doing Everyday Sustainability already, there is no real cost involved.

Since your customers may also include internal Stakeholders, people with inside information or suppliers with greater knowledge than the generic external customer, how do you manage the marketing and communications? My suggestion is that pragmatism should be the guide here: yes, they know about some of the warts (or all the warts), therefore nothing can be gained by hiding these facts. Instead, demonstrate a willingness to resolve these issues and communicate the progress. It goes without saying that any actions to improve the situation needs to be real, otherwise, trust will be replaced with even deeper cynicism, quickly.

Investors and shareholders will have more knowledge about you than the general public or your customers, but for them too, an ever-improving Energy Productivity KPI tells them that the organisation is well run and their investment is more likely to come good.

A coherent and consistent strategy to deal with uncertainty

When I started writing this book, we did not have Brexit, we did not have a negative result in the Italian referendum, we did not have the multiple options in a forthcoming French election; nor did we have North Korean submarines test firing ballistic missiles or an unexpected US election results. In other words, we did not have so much uncertainty.

This uncertainty often translates into a fear of the unknown, or what the near future appears to offer us. Uncertainty is usually seen as threats to many people, but you can also see uncertainty as opportunities – especially if your competitors are paralysed into endlessly analysing scenarios and options rather than acting decisively. Worse than the fear is the resultant paralysis, as people either have no idea what to do or procrastinate because they are waiting for the latest information that will complete the picture for them (which in uncertain times will probably not ever happen).

You can deal with the fear of change by looking at the facts: We don't know what is going to happen – predicting the future is rather difficult and such predictions are often unreliable. But to be paralysed by fear and indecision is even worse. By looking at the facts for activities we can control, we can make ourselves "ready" to deal with whatever is coming.

Devaluation of the currency? No big deal, especially if we minimise our costs through waste reduction. Price rises? We can deal with it if our processes are optimised both in resource usage and their deployment. Trade tariffs? We can still entice our customers if we offer a unique blend of value and added value through our technology deployment, our culture and work ethic and our managerial expertise.

Hey, isn't this Everyday Sustainability? Is this Doing More With Less? Of course it is; there is no real downside to this and not a lot to fear. It is probably the best way to go forward in a time of uncertainty – strengthen the internal processes and procedures, build a spirit of partnership and use whatever technologies we have optimally. We can have an organisation that stands a very good chance to see off possible threats and take advantage of any upcoming opportunities.

Notes

1 I was a metallurgist and the microscopes we used are more complex than the school biology class microscopes.
2 In Toyota's world, this approach is akin to fixing a problem with a car as it occurs during assembly rather than waiting for post-production inspection where the car will be taken apart to be fixed and then screwed together again, which may introduce additional errors and mistakes. Sorting things out at the right time and place not only saves time and costs, but also reduces the risk of more problems introduced later during the rework.
3 The term was apparently coined sometime in the 1960s by Peter Drucker, a management guru.
4 The 3R concept came from my previous book, *No Waste*, Gower, 2011.
5 Joseph Scanlon (1899–1956) was a steelworker, cost accountant, trades union officer, university lecturer and also a prize-fighter. He came up with the concept of a reward system linked to productivity Gains. He was clearly multi-skilled!
6 She developed the Lovelace List for Social Sustainability, see my book *No Waste* for more details. Contact Circle Three Consulting (www.circlethree.co.uk) for details of how your organisation can set up similar social enterprise initiatives.
7 *Financial Times*, 8 January 2017.

Appendix 1

Overall Effectiveness and the Energy Productivity KPI framework

In Chapter 2, I introduced the Energy Productivity Key Performance Indicator (KPI) and explained that it forms a framework for workplace effectiveness. We now explore this in much greater detail. Please note that the techniques described below are explored further in Appendix 2.

I suggest that you use the Overall Effectiveness measure as an approach towards improving Energy Productivity. This comprises three elements, as described earlier in the book: the Availability of the resources and assets, the Performance of the available resources and assets and the Quality of the outputs. These are examined below in terms of effectiveness and efficiency as well as their underlying contributing factors. As quality is generally a more familiar concept in business; I will focus more on Availability and Performance.

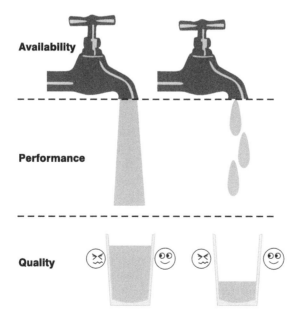

Figure A1.1 Components of Overall Effectiveness – Example.

It is possible to view the relationships between the three elements of Overall Effectiveness as shown in Figure A1.1. The tap example showed that if Availability is reduced by closing the tap, then it will impact directly on Performance, as the flow rate will drop. Quality is an independent variable in that only the quantity of the output is affected. Nevertheless, in a real-world business situation, a lower output means not meeting specifications.

Availability of the resources and assets

The concept is quite straightforward: If the resources are not available, then they cannot deliver outcomes or values. This can be extended to partially available resources and assets too, for example: if you have a toothache, it makes concentration much harder, and it is likely that you will get less done that day. Similarly, if a photocopier keeps jamming, copies cannot be made quickly and therefore its value delivery will be lower. This can also be applied to people with the wrong skills or people who are just too busy to devote the time needed to do a job properly.

Efficient management of the Availability KPI is about using only the necessary resources and assets to deliver the designed outcomes. This is like just-in-time delivery[1] where, theoretically, you get what you need exactly. In reality, constraints on the amount in each batch will mean exact may not be exact and most people also like to be sure in case of errors and mistakes, so there is some over-ordering. This concern about having enough to do the job brings us to the Effectiveness aspects of the Availability KPI.

Effective management of Availability is about achieving the targets; therefore, the right resources and assets must be there. This is not about the right amounts, but about delivering the goods. So we may have the right number of people in the team, but if they do not have the right skills to deliver the job, then their Effectiveness will be poor, even if the Efficiency outcome is great.

Availability is reliant on scheduling and maintenance. For equipment and material resources, this is about making sure that the right amount or numbers are in the plan and within the budget. But careful planning isn't just about the right numbers, for example: a construction company working near Bristol got some 360° excavators through an auction sight unseen (to save money, I would guess, although I was told the official reason was to save time) and although they had the right number of excavators on site, these broke down so frequently that the project ran late. So a supposed economic decision ended up costing more and failing to deliver both efficiency and effectiveness.

For inputs, whether materials or information, keeping the Availability KPI high is about good organisation; it is about thinking of materials as part of a flow rather than a single discrete action. Therefore, the movement of materials and information needs to be optimised with transfer routes, storage, labelling and retrieval all thought through. In practice, carrying out a 5S campaign at the materials storage locations will enhance storage and retrievals. These activities can be further optimised by exploring and eliminating opportunities for problems: for example, I advised a sterilisation unit in a hospital to cover the sharp corners on the shelves and trolleys in their area to avoid tearing the wrapped and sterilised trays of instruments for the operating theatres. Simple individual activities like these can only help raise the Availability KPI incrementally, but over the course of time and many repetitions, such as in a hospital, the gains can be quite significant.

Besides deploying workplace organisation, or 5S, another useful analysis is Suppliers, Inputs, Process, Outputs and Customers (SIPOC): by examining the immediate upstream and downstream steps, a team can work out and optimise the way materials and information are handled and stored.

Asset or equipment maintenance is a matter of partnership, with the operator being the front line inspector. There is a mantra from Total Productive Maintenance that goes something like this: "In maintenance, cleaning leads to spotting, spotting leads to fixing." This was to encourage the operators to keep the work area and equipment clean and tidy, thus making it easy to spot and fix minor problems.

Availability of people is a different matter because it is not necessarily controllable by better planning, scheduling or asset maintenance. As described earlier, if you are not there, you can't deliver, if you are there but not really engaged, you are unlikely to be fully delivering either. For people, Availability can be about keeping yourself physically in a position to deliver your targets.

Some companies take the view that these Availability drops are part of the cost of doing business, and many, therefore, are working on the basis of a number of sick days per employees per year.[2] In terms of Energy Productivity, it is a balance between the loss of resources and an excessive level of resources. In an austerity climate, you can image which approach companies will take. The other problem with the number of people in Energy Productivity calculations is that the Systems Energy requirements for the company do not necessarily drop if one of your team is having a day off, sick.

Another aspect about sickness at work linked to Availability is that some organisations think they need to offer an attractive sick days/duvet days package to attract top employees. In these situations, it is about achieving a level of productivity that is acceptable with the extra value brought by these top employees.

Contract employees can be deployed as buffers and safety resources, and, similarly, there are companies offering tool and equipment hire. But then you get the problem of unfamiliarity with the work or unfamiliarity with the equipment and their impacts on the process Performance aspects.

However, many people also go absent from work (perhaps in their minds, with the bodies still being around) because they are not particularly engaged or they reckon they can get away with it. Either way, the problem can be attributed to a lack of motivation as well as various wellbeing issues. In this book, I proposed considering Respect, Recognition and Rewards as the ways forwards to address people and their engagement. But there is also a set of

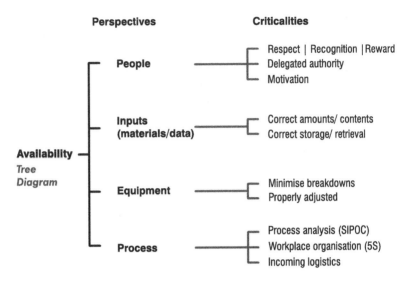

Figure A1.2   Availability Tree Diagram.

deeper empowerment issues that can help motivate people: this is about delegating authority for problem solving and implementing solutions to the people doing the job.

I suggest that a supervisor or a manager needs to be there, but mainly to coach and facilitate, rather than to direct. By framing the delegated authority carefully, a perimeter can be set within where the staff can innovate and thence become more engaged. If the perimeter is set as in the following example: "We have a problem moving material in our work area, how can we tackle that?"; then the team's authority to change is limited to a particular part of the process. Should the team decide that it is necessary to engage upstream or downstream activities, then the manager or supervisor can then act to facilitate discussions and dialogues. In these instances, the more engaged team can probably come up with a more efficient and effective deployment of people resources should a team member becomes unwell.

In summary: to enhance the Availability factor, try the following, as outlined in Figure A1.2 – the Tree Diagram for Criticalities that impact the Availability KPI.

Performance of the resources

We often assume in planning that people, materials and equipment will be working as designed – with the necessary knowledge, the right amount and at the right pace. However, in reality, we know that is often not true. In fact, we have project plans that take into account delays and process maps that show reiterations. Then there are materials with different characteristics although supposedly from the same batch.[3] Nonetheless, Performance is something we tend to take for granted generally: When you buy a new TV, you expect it to work more or less like what you expect a TV to do. It is probably because we lack the correct benchmarks that allow some Performance problems to slip through. Therefore, often without adequate information, we design systems and processes to work at a certain pace that we assume will allow us to meet our customers' needs and demands.

Performance issues can be divided into inadequate information, inadequate skills and inadequate management, as well as inadequate Available resources to achieve the targets.

In the case of technology and its deployment, the Performance KPI can appear to adopt more conservative thinking: avoid cutting-edge technology and wait until the teething problems have been ironed out. However, this can mean losing a certain amount of competitive advantage as a follower rather than a leader. A more pragmatic approach would be to pilot new technology thoroughly to identify potential problems as opposed to rushing to be first. An organisational culture where issues can be openly discussed is also helpful as it can avoid both *group think* and *group shift* – respectively, where conformity leads to a team to seek consensus and avoid individual views and when the team takes on greater risks collectively in areas where individuals would be more risk aversive.

A more day-to-day approach towards enhancing Performance in equipment is to eliminate minor stoppages and slow running. Both of these can arise from poor maintenance regimes, and, once again, the equipment operator acts as the first line maintenance by observing and reporting on-going performance as well as rectifying minor issues before they grow to large problems.

Managing the level of inputs, whether materials or information, is also important in maintaining a high Performance KPI. It is, however, more than the just-in-time approach in the Availability KPI, because not only do the inputs need to be there, they also need to be in a place where their retrieval and usage is easy, simple and practical. Essentially, such resources need to be easily retrieved for use, with packaging that is simple to open (whether physical or as digital data) as well as practical to handle and locate. For example, in cooking, many cooks place measured amounts of ingredients in readily accessible containers closer to hand – a place for everything and everything in its place. It is known as *mis en place* in cooking (and related to 5S in operations management).

Conventional thinking would attribute improving Performance in people as being dependent both on skills and on workplace organisation. Training and development establishes a worker's capabilities in current and future work. Nowadays, the hype about knowledge workers tends to hide the fact that nearly every type of work requires knowledge, and an experienced worker usually has the ability to do it better. Notice, however, that I have now introduced the words knowledge and experience – these are not necessarily the same as competence or capability. We now have four aspects that are linked to skills as described in Figure A1.3.

Theoretical knowledge is all very well and virtually anyone can gain that, but practising and using the knowledge is more beneficial as value is being delivered. Through repetition and correcting mistakes, we start to gain experience, and through improving, we become competent. Therefore, mere skills training does not deliver full value on its own, as there also need to be development and growth for an individual to become competent. Nonetheless, this type of training and development clearly has a cost, although this will be more than recovered if the individual is allowed to use the skills to improve the process or to innovate. Unfortunately, this is an area that many employers tend to neglect, as they feel that in the short term (especially during tough times), training can be cut without immediate impacts, and they often further argue that their workforce is transient or readily replaceable. But gains in performance do require nurturing, and without an investment, not a lot will happen. This was also explored briefly in Chapter 4 and in Figure 4.6.

The other area where people and behaviour can impact Performance is the physical workspace. This is where ergonomics and other design aspects play a role. In general, if the working environment is pleasant, things tend to go better. Now, what is pleasant for me may not be so for you, but generally a clean and reasonably tidy workplace with clean air, low noise levels and good lighting is welcoming. This, however, needs to be balanced with workplace safety and also the flow of materials in the working process. These

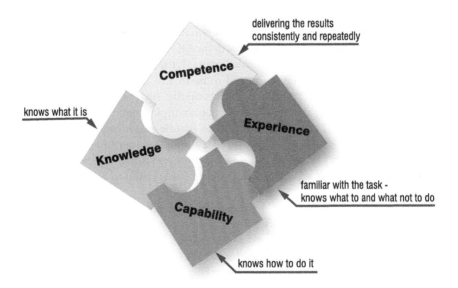

Figure A1.3 Skills: The Components.

workspace-related actions are all value enabling and therefore, incur a cost, which means they need to be optimised.

Process improvements lead to Performance gains. This is the conventional thinking and quite often the conventional truth. However, this only works if the improvements are properly analysed and implemented; good intentions on their own are not sufficient. In Lean manufacturing, two sets of methods are deployed to add value to Performance; they are *Poka Yoke* and Single-Minute Exchange of Dies (SMED) (see Appendix 2). *Poka Yoke* is about making sure all the necessary elements to complete the process are in place such that all the steps are taken in the right sequence. A checklist comes to mind for many of us in our work activities. SMED is also about getting ready for work – simplifying and making sure everything is ready for the main work activity. A third technique, Visual Management, is aimed at enabling value and offering more rapid checks of progress, outcomes as well as status information.

To make this happen, we should "go and see" (*gemba*): We need to go where the action is taking place and observe what is going on and what is hindering Performance. A detailed Value Stream Map can then be developed and Performance choke points identified, evaluated, analysed and addressed.

Often, Performance improvements come from a combination of people and process. For example, a hospital in London looked at the transport of patients between wards and treatment and optimised two elements of the process: cutting the bureaucracy of the transport documentation and making the porter a partner in the transport rather than just a mechanism for patient

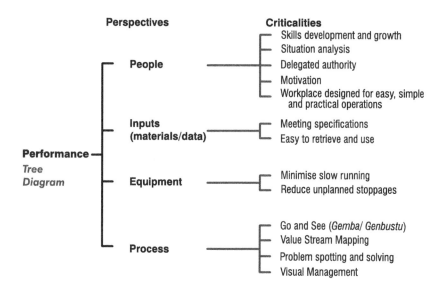

Figure A1.4 Performance Tree Diagram.

delivery. So instead of being told to move a patient and doing it with inadequate information (since people were too busy to spend seven minutes to fill in a transport form), the porters now sign the newly designed, clear and short transport document when they collect the patient and then again sign off when they arrive at the destination. This reassured the hospital's insurers such that it resulted in reduced insurance costs.

In summary, to enhance Performance, you can explore the following, as shown in Figure A1.4, the Tree Diagram outlining the Criticalities in this area.

Quality of the outputs

This is often the most familiar of the Overall Effectiveness KPIs, but there are some particular issues that are linked with both actual and perceived quality that need to be taken into account.

A motivated workforce is often assumed to deliver higher quality; this may be because we observe the enthusiasm of the employees and relate this to "employees who cares" and perhaps subconsciously attach "… about quality" to the end of our observation. Anecdotes and observations often confirm this, but enthusiasm alone does not result in quality. Skills (knowledge, etc.) combined with knowing how to analyse situations can result in a reduction of quality variations, but only if it comes with delegated authority to make the local decisions.

Materials and data inputs not only need to match the specifications, but the specifications need to be correct and, ideally, selected for enhanced quality. Sure, this may cost more, but you need to decide which level of quality meets with your customers' and users' needs. A cheaper set of inputs, whether materials or data, may require different processing to get the full value. While this appears more relevant for materials, information from somewhat unreliable sources will need additional checks to ensure it is fit for use in a professional organisation.

Having the right equipment settings can reduce variations, but only if the equipment is well maintained such that you can trust the outputs produced are as per the settings.[4] When information forms the inputs, then the maintenance is making sure your assessment skills are up-to-date so that you can judge whether the inputs are likely to be useful, troublesome or false, as in false news.

There are numerous approaches towards improving quality; in fact there is an entire industry that provides you with advice and services.

Improve quality by minimising variations: Analyse the opportunities for variations in the process, and resolve those through improvements. However, since quality also has a perception element, then the steps after processing need to be considered. This is shown in Figure A1.5.

The main elements of the post-process steps are: dispatch, reception/retrieval, use and any subsequent service and/or maintenance. Perceptions of

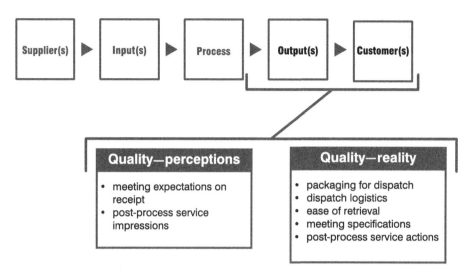

Figure A1.5 Quality Elements Post-Processing.

quality appear in each of these areas: Were the outputs dispatched on time? Were they in a good condition when we received them? Could we access the outputs easily? If there were problems, how were they resolved? Addressing these relies on interpersonal skills with our customers/users as well as paying attention to details regarding the dispatch and logistics. Sometimes, of course, you just cannot win: You packed the parcel very well to minimise damages only to receive a feedback of "excessive packaging." You send the file in the latest format with all the wizzo capabilities only for your user to say that their software was three versions older and could not access your file. This is where the interpersonal aspects come in – charm them and fix the problem.

Actual quality is more about meeting specifications; this can also raise problems if your customer was not clear enough in the original specifications or they simply got the specifications wrong. As long as you fulfilled your part in meeting the specifications, then it is not your problem. Nevertheless, to enhance the perception of quality, you should accommodate them somewhat. However, the Energy Productivity impacts need to be taken into account, as this is essentially a rework situation.

In summary, you may wish to explore the following as outlined in Figure A1.6 – the Tree Diagram for Criticalities that impact the Quality KPI.

This is a short explanation of the factors that contribute to the Overall Effectiveness components in the Energy Productivity KPI. These components can also be expressed using a What/How Matrix, as shown in Figure A1.7.

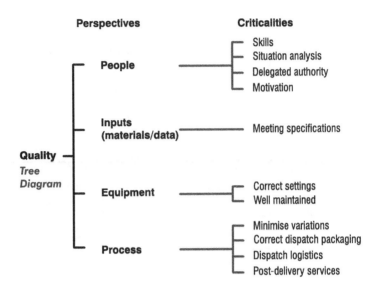

Figure A1.6 Quality Tree Diagram.

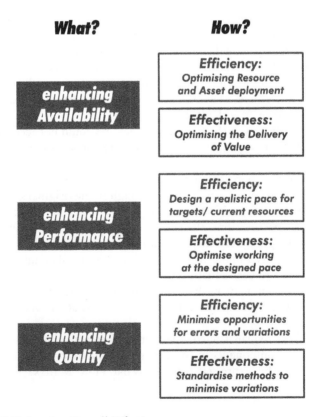

Figure A1.7 Enhancing Overall Effectiveness.

Notes

1 A major Lean concept; see Appendix 2 for more details.
2 Other employers have "duvet days", when you can call in to take the day off with no questions asked. This is an employee benefit that came from the US, and apparently participating companies plan for up to four such days per year.
3 Such as the four white door panels on my bedroom wardrobe: they all aged differently, resulting in four distinctly different shades of off-white after a few years...
4 I often wondered whether my oven at home is really working at the temperature set on the dial...

Appendix 2

Glossary and descriptions of the tools and techniques

This glossary is divided into sections to describe the various jargon, tools and techniques described in my book. Neither the lists nor the contents are meant to be exhaustive. Additional reading is suggested where relevant.

The following is a short list of Business, Management and Marketing tools that are useful in any analysis (see Table A2.1). Virtually all of these can work as an analysis framework: You can stick each of these within any other tool and carry out a thorough analysis, for example:

1 Putting the Balance Scorecard perspectives as elements within each of the four Strengths, Weaknesses, Opportunities and Threats (SWOT) analysis parameters – strength from our finances, strength of our customers, strength of our staff and strength from our process, etc.

2 When using the Marketing Mix, look at the SWOT for each of the Price, Product, Promotion and Place (4Ps) elements: What is our strength in Product? What is our strength in Promotion? What opportunity is available in Place? Etc.

Table A2.1 Jargon for Business, Management and Marketing

Jargon	Plain English (as much as possible)
SWOT analysis	• The SWOT analysis stands for an analysis of the Strengths, Weaknesses, Opportunities and Threats. It can be applied to almost any organisation, department, team or individual. Its popularity stems from its universal applicability and that it does not require extensive training to use it effectively. • The SWOT analysis is a two-part approach in that the Strengths and Weaknesses are internal issues to the company whereas the Opportunities and Threats are usually external factors. • Its origins are unclear, but the memorable acronym has been in use since 1966.

(Continued)

Jargon	*Plain English (as much as possible)*
PEST analysis	• PEST stands for Political, Economic, Social and Technological. It is the external analysis that describes factors that shape a business environment. • PEST has suffered inflation since it first appeared in the mid-1960s: extra parameters have been successively added: Legal (to SLEPT) then Environmental (to PESTEL), then Ethical (to STEEPLE) and then Demographical (to STEEPLED). I have no idea why this is so; I can only imagine consultant and academic one up-manship.
Balanced Scorecard	• The Balanced Scorecard was developed by Kaplan and Norton in 1992 as a response to the singular emphasis placed on financial returns by the major companies then. The Balanced Scorecard suggests focussing equally on four perspectives in an organisation: its Finances, its Customers, its Processes and the development and growth of its Staff. • This has since caught on in a big way, as it offers a very flexible yet complete framework for analysis. • The Balanced Scorecard should not be confused with the plan "balanced scorecard" – the latter is any business scorecard that offers a balanced approach to viewing the critical parameters of that particular business.
Triple Bottom Line	• This is a balanced scorecard (note no capitals) developed by John Elkington in 1994 that takes into account the Environmental issues alongside Economic/Financial and Social issues as part of an organisation's management framework. • This is often described colloquially as People/Planet/Profit. The order of the three words is often used to demonstrate your particular loyalties; mine is alphabetical!
Marketing Mix	• This is a marketing tool also called the 4Ps: Product, Price, Place and Promotion. It provides a balanced scorecard of sorts to describe a marketing and communications message. • Product – Essentially, what is the utility and value from the product or service • Price – The physical costs as well as the intangible costs like learning curve, behaviour change required etc. • Place – Where can people get hold of the product/service? Physically? Online? What about logistics? Etc. • Promotion – How do we shape the message to tell people about this? • The 4P Marketing Mix also suffered from inflation; it is now 8P with Physical environment, People, Productivity and quality and Process. I have no idea what the new parameters mean. I found the original 4Ps sufficient on all the occasions I needed to use it.
Switching Costs	• This is a set of costs that is associated with changing behaviour. It is assumed that when you change behaviour, there are costs involved.

Jargon	*Plain English (as much as possible)*

- It can be tangible: a physical price you pay for the new product/service; the time taken to learn how to use the new product service; the physical changes you are required to make in your workplace (real or computer) to accommodate the new product/service.
- There may even a physical termination cost when switching from one product/service contract to another.
- It can also be intangible, such as the behaviour change you need to make to switch from one type of behaviour to another: the need to remember doing things a different way or to do different things. The intangible termination costs can also be high. People tend to be nostalgic about the "good old days," which makes change even more difficult.

Further reading for business and management topics are difficult to suggest, as there are so many available.

However, a quick search on the Internet will provide you with a large volume of information varying from useful to amusing.

For the purist, Kaplan and Norton's original publication of the Balanced Scorecard was in the January/February 1992 issue of the *Harvard Business Review*. Elkington's Triple Bottom Line appeared in the Winter 1994 issue of the *California Management Review*.

Improvement techniques

I mentioned many Lean, Six Sigma, Total Productive Maintenance and other Quality-related tools and techniques in the book; the background of these are described briefly below.

Lean

Lean comes from the Toyota Production System (TPS) and is based on eliminating waste and improving process flow. Toyota has been developing and evolving the TPS since the early 1950s, and its principles have been adopted by manufacturing, services and healthcare organisations around the world. Its concepts are likely to be at the core of most progressive business operations (see Table A2.2).

Further reading on Lean can be accessed either via the Lean classics listed below or through the Internet.

Ohno's *Toyota Production System* from Productivity Press, 1988 is the original source for Lean, whereas the books by Womack and Jones made Lean accessible to the West (they coin the term Lean). These include: *The Machine that Changed the World*, and *Lean Thinking*. Liker's *Toyota Way* from is a useful practitioner's guide.

Table A2.2 Jargon for Lean

Jargon	Plain English (as much as possible)
5S/Can Do	• This is a methodology for organising the workplace to become more efficient and effective as well as safer. The 5 "S"s come from Japanese words with an "S" sound. Various Western interpretations include acronyms like CAN DO.

Japanese	5S	5C	CAN DO/ ANCOD
Seri	Sort	Clear Out	Arrange
Seiton	Set	Configure	Neatness
Seiso	Shine	Clean & Check	Cleanliness
Seiketsu	Shine	Conformity	Order
Shitsuki	Sustain	Custom & Practice	Discipline

	• As you can see, none of these are particular wonderful translations, with CAN DO being particularly hard on non-native English speakers ("… but the sequence is ANCOD, so why…")
5 Whys	• This is the Root Cause analysis: By asking "Why?" 5 times, you should be able to reach the Root Cause of the problem. If you cannot get to the Root Cause, then perhaps your initial definition is a bit too broad.
7 or 8 Wastes	• This is originally from Toyota's Hidden Factory concept where all the waste resides. However, we don't notice them as we see them every day and they become a part of the scenery. This is a major concept in Lean.
	• I added an eighth: waste – wasted talent and ideas from the workforce – into the original seven wastes and modified some of these to reflect a more general non-manufacturing usage
A3	• This is a report based on an A3 sheet format. The left side describes the issue and the right side describes the way forward. Its usefulness stems from the limited size of the sheet, which discourages waffling.
	• An A3-sized sheet was the largest sheet Toyota could send through a fax machine, hence the name.
Andon	• This is a system of signal lights/cords in Toyota factories – where a worker can pull the cord to stop the production line to fix a quality problem on the spot. Now used as a generic signal in visual management.
Buffer and Safety Resources	• Buffer Resources are deployed when customer order patterns vary – like during a sale.
	• Safety Resources are deployed when the process is disrupted due to internal constraints (i.e. screw-ups) or inefficiencies (i.e. other screw-ups).
Cause-Effect analysis (Fishbone analysis)	• This is also known as the Fishbone analysis (on account of its shape) or Ishikawa diagrams. It is a team-based tool to ascertain the most likely cause of a problem by observing and voting on the most likely outcomes under a range of general causal categories.

Jargon	*Plain English (as much as possible)*
	• Often, a set of Common Causes is used; these are: external events, tools, materials, skills, methods and communications.
Flow	• This is the nirvana of Lean operations. It is about every piece of work moving along only due to customer demand. In other words, no over-production of buffer stock. This is linked to a supply chain that manages Just-in-Time deliveries. A quick reality check tells us that somewhere along the line, someone has to hold stocks to deal with fluctuating demands from customers. Like all nirvanas, it is easier to talk about them than to achieve them.
Gemba	• This is a Japanese word meaning the "now place;" in other words, where the work/action is taking place. It is used to indicate that it is always better to go and see what is going on than guessing.
Genbustu	• This is a Japanese word meaning the "real thing" (and not the fizzy drink) – it is about the actual events happening at the "now place."
Heijunka	• This is a Japanese phrase that means "workload levelling," a very critical factor in manufacturing that allows "flow." This is also about a balanced workload between different lines, during a standard work period etc.
Hoshin Kanri	• This is a Japanese phrase that literally means "compass management," but has been taken by its boosters to mean strategic direction. It can be simplified to the PDCA cycle.
Jidoka	• This is a Japanese phrase about "machines with a human touch," semi-automatic machines that have sensors to provide information on their operating environment. An equally illuminating English translation is "Autonomation" (this is a word made up by Toyota).
Just-in-Time	• This is the core of Toyota production system. It is about getting supplies in just when you need it to avoid over stocking and keep the "flow" going smoothly. This worked well until awful external events like the 1975 earthquake in Japan disrupted Toyota's very lean Just-in-Time system and left the factories with no raw materials for production.
Kaizen	• This is Japanese phrase meaning "correction;" it is now a generic term for improvement or continuous improvement.
Kanban	• This Japanese word means "signal." It is used in Just-in-Time systems to indicate that the stock is running low and a new batch is needed. The original Kanbans are cardboard sheets with the relevant part number details. Nowadays, supermarkets use the bar codes as a signal to track sales and to send reorder information.
Muda	• This means "waste;" Toyota aficionados elaborate with Type 1 (pure waste) and Type 2 (value-enabling) wastes. For the rest of us, *muda* is plain waste – of the seven waste types.

(Continued)

Jargon	*Plain English (as much as possible)*
	• For the purpose of this book, I combined the eight wastes with *mura* and *muri* below to form 10 Common Wastes. (Yes, I contribute to inflation of management jargon too!)
Mura	• This means "stripes" literally, or unevenness in production flow. Or it is used to describe variation, as when different groups of people do the same job but in different ways.
	• A good example is when you ring up a call centre about the same subject on two separate occasions; you are likely to get different answers.
Muri	• This means "pointless" or "no reason" literally. It is about pointless activities carried out at work that does not add value.
	• Contacting a call centre is also likely to be a relevant example here, but let's move on.
PDCA/PDSA	• This is the Deming improvement cycle: Plan-Do-Check/Study-Act. It is the basis of every quality improvement (or any improvement) programme.
	• Deming is a statistics guru who strongly influenced Japan's production ethos in the post-1945 period.
Poka-Yoke	• This is a Japanese phrase meaning "fool-proofing." It means designing a method/procedure/product that is essentially difficult to get wrong.
	• Originally the phrase is *baka yoke* or idiot proofing, but political correctness (and perhaps an acceptance of reality) put paid to that.
	• A checklist is a very good example of *Poka Yoke*.
Pull/Push	• This is a piece of Toyota philosophy that says we should respond to customer demand (and let them pull our products) instead of giving customers what we (think they) want – or push.
	• A good example is the modern sandwich shops selling pre-packaged sandwiches (vendor Push) versus the old fashion sandwich shop where they make it to your order (customer Pull).
Shadow Boards	• This is a Lean visual management element where outlines of tools are sprayed onto a board so everyone can see where the tool should be stored.
SMED	• This acronym means "Single Minute Exchange of Die" – it stems from changing the dies in hydraulic presses that stamp out car body parts. Generally, it means to have a very effective changeover on a single piece of machinery. Toyota managed (after several years) to get the changeover of its massive dies to less than 10 minutes when General Motors was taking up to four hours or more.
	• A more accurate acronym should be UMED for Unit Minute Exchange of Die (i.e. less than two digits or 1–9) but that is just being pedantic.

Jargon	*Plain English (as much as possible)*
	• Basically this is about optimising the process by getting everything ready such that the most important element of the process is least delayed. A good example is the tyre change in Formula One car racing; a large team of mechanics get everything/everyone in place to change four wheels in about two seconds – minimising the stop time of the most crucial element – the racing car.
Takt time	• *Takt* is a German word to describe the metronome's movement. It is used by Toyota to describe the time needed to produce one unit of output. It forms the basis of the production schedule.
Visual Management	• This is a system of signals and information that helps the teams at work by providing unambiguous details.
	• Examples can include notice boards, Shadow Boards and production information displayed overhead at the line.
VSM	• This stands for Value Stream Mapping and is a critical Lean tool to analyse the production process. It tracks the value adding in any process and lists the necessary variables to allow for effective management or improvement.
	• Some people (mostly project managers) see VSM as a (very) high-level Process Map.

Six Sigma Quality

Six Sigma is a statistical concept where quality is at 99.99966 per cent or 3.4 defects per 1 million opportunities. It was developed by Motorola in the late 1980s in its multi-phase, multi-component circuit board fabrication. A major booster was General Electric (GE) who claimed "billions" in savings. By the late 1990s, it became the go-to process improvement. Six Sigma is heavy on the number-crunching statistical analysis. I have made the decision to leave these areas out of this book as they are more aimed at quality professionals and not the rest of us.

The Six Sigma movement was also quite effective in claiming various existing tools under its umbrella; these are therefore listed below to make life easier for everyone (see Table A2.3).

Suggesting further reading in Six Sigma is getting difficult, as there are so many available in the field now. Again, try the Internet and also have a look at some of the many books available and see what takes your fancy. Be aware that first, some of these books actually contain errors (clearly those publishers did not meet the Six Sigma standard) and secondly, not all the books list all the useful tools and techniques.

However, a very complete House of Quality book is the one by Ficalora and Cohen: *Quality Function Deployment and Six Sigma*.

Table A2.3 Jargon for Six Sigma

Jargon	Plain English (as much as possible)
DMAIC	• This stands for Define/Measure/Analyse/ Improve/Control and is the standard Six Sigma approach towards problem solving. Each of these five steps can encompass a number of analytical tools, thus making DMAIC a tool framework.
FMEA	• Failure Modes and Effects Analysis is a structured way to examine how a process, product or service can fail. It analyses to examine both the risks of failure and mitigation activities. For our purposes, it can be seen as a risk assessment on steroids. Essentially, the FMEA is based on the severity, the likelihood and the detectability of a particular risk.
	• It has been around since 1980 but now often considered as part of Six Sigma.
	• An extended discussion on some of the issues relating to FMEA is available at the end of this glossary.
House of Quality (HoQ)	• This is a quality management framework or mega tool. It has the reputation of being the most complex quality management tool. It is made up of a number of matrices (from, say, seven upwards to perhaps 23). The House of Quality was invented at Mitsubishi Shipyards in designing oil tankers in the 1970s. It too pre-dates Six Sigma.
	• This is also known as Quality Function Deployment, where the requirements and solutions (the What/How) cascade towards ever more detail, and you will probably end up with individual unit activities, which then allow you to work out the time and cost more accurately. I personally think it may also drown you in information.
	• The core of the HoQ is the relationships or impact matrix. It is where the needs or requirements are matched with the proposed solutions.
	• An extended discussion on using the HoQ to develop a strategy, such as an Everyday Sustainability strategy, is provided in Appendix 3.
Process Mapping	• This has been around for many years, but it allows assessment of the causes of variations in a process, so many people now consider it as part of the Six Sigma toolbox.
SIPOC	• Supplier(s)/Input(s)/Process/Output(s)/ Customer(s): This is a process analysis for a single process step and is very detailed in order to assist in analysing for the causes of variations.

Table A2.4 TPM Jargon

Jargon	Plain English (as much as possible)
Overall Equipment Effectiveness (OEE)	• OEE is derived from multiplying the asset Availability rate, asset Performance rate and output Quality rate. World-class status is generally reckoned to have an OEE of 85 per cent or higher. The aim is to achieve Availability at 90 per cent, Performance at 95 per cent and Quality at 99 per cent.
Six Major Losses	• These are: equipment breakdowns and adjustments (Availability issues); minor stoppages and slow running (Performance issues); and start up instabilities and rework/scrap (Quality issues).
Eight Pillars of TPM	• The 8 pillars, to me, is more a philosophical basis for TPM where the two described above are more practical for everyday use. The pillars are: • Focussed Improvement • Autonomous maintenance • Planned Maintenance • Quality maintenance • Cost Deployment • Early Equipment Management • Training and Education • Safety Health Environment

Total Productive Maintenance

TPM was developed by the Denso Corporation in Japan, and it described the concept of Overall Equipment Effectiveness. So far as I can ascertain, it has three main tool concepts (see Table A2.4).

TPM has a more limited further reading selection: *TPM* by Willmott; *Total Productive Maintenance* by Rich and *Lean TPM* by McCarthy and Rich. These are all practitioner books, by the way.

Other quality and improvement tools/techniques

The quality tools listed below appears to come from Japan – I am not too sure whether they are invented by Japanese quality engineers, but they were certainly packaged in a coherent way by Professor Ishikawa, the inventor of quality circles, in the 1950s.

The two sets of tools are not new to us now, and many of us use them without thinking, as they are very logical, but back in the day, they were the starting point tools for any meaningful analysis (see Table A2.5).

Generally, there are many documents and books for further reading. However, a very good source is the American Society for Quality (ASQ). Needless to say, this is likely to cost money. *The Quality Toolbox* by Tague, published by the ASQ is a good reference with virtually all the quality tools in one book.

Table A2.5 Jargon for Quality

Jargon	Plain English (as much as possible)
Seven Basic Tools	It is claimed that Ishikawa compiled these after he was inspired by a talk given by Edwards Deming (of the Deming quality fame) in the 1950s. They are: 1 Cause and Effect diagram (the fishbone/Ishikawa diagram). 2 Check Sheet – A structured table to allow the input of information suitable for analysis. 3 Control Charts – Charts to show how a process changes with time. 4 Histograms – This shows how often a set of data appears – we see this as a bar graph or a pie chart. 5 Pareto chart – This graphs shows which factors are more significant. We also call this the lever rule, or 80-20 rule. 6 Scatter diagram – This pairs numerical data to allow us to interpret relationships; examples are any X-Y or Y-time charts. 7 Stratification – This separates data into segments so that patterns can be seen.
Seven Management and Planning Tools	In 1976, the Japan Union of Scientists and Engineers saw the need for new quality tools, and these were developed. Again, not all are new but their compilation into a group and promotion as a group saw their use soar. 1 Affinity diagram – This organises information into naturally related groups 2 Relations diagram – This is the cause and effect analysis in a tabulated diagram form, allowing more complex relationships to be analysed. 3 Tree Diagram – This is the opposite of the Affinity diagram, as it breaks down an issue into more specific elements. 4 Matrix diagram – This shows the relationship between two or more groups of information and how they interact. This is essentially the What/How relationship described in the book. 5 Prioritisation matrix – How different elements interact with each other; a part of the House of Quality. (This has replaced the original tool on the list – matrix data analysis) 6 Arrow diagram – This shows the order of activities in a process. Essentially this is the basis of project plans, process maps etc. 7 Process decision program chart – This is mainly a process map, but with inputs details, outputs details, function analysis as well as a failure mode analysis.

The Likert Scale

There is one other tool that I described in this book, and that is the five-point scale for ranking just about everything. This 1 for low and 5 for high scale has a real name: It is a Likert-type Scale and widely used in responses to surveys. In the five-point scale, the scoring is as follows:

1   Low
2   Middle to Low
3   Middle
4   Middle to High
5   High

I choose the 1–5 scale because it is a lot easier to differentiate than in the 10-point Likert scale. There are a few points to remember about using this tool:

*   Always use an odd number of points to make analysis easier
*   This is a good way of converting a simple yes/no answer into a range, which then allows some statistical analysis
*   You can do some serious voodoo analysis using the Likert numbers – it is how I reckon the advertisers come up with nine out of 10 cats prefer a particular brand of cat food.

Using the Likert Scale results is quite simple: you present the data, say for a list of risks in FMEA (see below) in a series of 1–5 responses, and then you can compare them like for like in each of the three FMEA factors. Another way to explore Likert-type results is to compare the results from different people/ teams – Why is there a discrepancy in the results? – then you can explore the reasons why the results are different.

The Likert Scale is not a sophisticated tool, but the ways you can analyse the outcomes can be quite valuable.

Additional note on FMEA

Failure Mode Effects Analysis (FMEA) was originally developed by the US military in the 1980s as a Military Standard[1]. While it is a very useful tool, there are several issues about its use you should be aware of.

One is a bit of a dispute about whether multiplying the three FMEA factors of severity, likelihood and detectability is the most accurate way of analysis. In conventional FMEA, a scoring of 1–10 is used for each of the three factors. A Risk Probability Number (RPN) is calculated by multiplying the three factors, and then the risks are ranked and prioritised. However, multiplying 10×10×10 gives 1,000 outcomes, and it means a large range of factor combinations can share the same RPN, as shown in Table A2.6.

Table A2.6 Same Risk Probability Number (360) for Different Combinations of Issues

	Severity	*Likelihood*	*Detectability*
Example 1	very, very high – 10	very high – 9	quite easy – 4
Example 2	quite low – 4	very high – 9	impossible – 10
Example 3	moderate – 6	moderate – 6	impossible – 10

My suggestion for an easier-to-use FMEA method is as follows:

1   Rely on real data to help you decide the scoring (when you are designing something, use historical data to help);
2   Use a 1–5 scale instead of 1–10, since I can never tell "moderately easy" and "quite easy" apart; and
3   Assess the risk and score on a 1–5 scale based on your experience, knowledge and instinct[2].
4   Add the three factors instead of multiplying them; so instead of 1,000 outcomes, you have (only) 125 to deal with (5×5×5).
5   Carry out a Reality Check[3] to make sure the risk scoring makes sense in the real world and is based on observation (i.e. not guesswork).

The other argument about FMEA is what happens when the three parameters are put together as a Risk Priority Number or risk ranking. Now, the argument goes like this: Severity, Likelihood and Detectability are unrelated parameters, so adding (or multiplying) three discrete unrelated parameters gives you nonsense.

Put another way, you can add three bananas, two oranges and five apples together to get 10 pieces of fruit, as all three have a common link, which is that they are all fruit. Now, try it again with bananas, nails and rubber ducks and you can see what the arguments about the FMEA parameters are about. There is nothing really linking severity, likelihood and detectability together as it stands, and therefore, the RPN has no meaning.

Having said that, the RPN is still a useful number to give an indication of the degree of impacts from the risk. I have personally used it in applications for grants (and was successful too!). But it really is not good form, so my recommendation is to put all three into a framework where they can be linked. A simple approach is to put these in terms of costs incurred: If this risk happened and it is severe, it will cost us £x; if it happened and it is severe but we did not detect it in time, it will cost us £y. Then a set of RPN can be expressed in comparable terms.

Notes

1   Mil STD 1629A – Procedures for performing a failure mode, effects and criticality analysis, Department of Defense, USA 1980.
2   Yes, the scoring is subjective, but you can mitigate this by discussing with others working in the area as well as using data to achieve a consensus. Ultimately, it is your judgement and if you are not sure, ask someone.
3   This is the technical term for "for goodness sake, use some common sense."

Appendix 3
The House of Quality and developing a strategy

Establishing a coherent and consistent strategy often means a systematic way of working out the way forward. But, it does not necessarily mean that inspirations are stifled. I believe that the House of Quality (HoQ) technique fits the requirements of developing a strategy in a coherent and comprehensive framework, as suggested in Chapter 10. This is achieved by linking needs, capabilities and corporate constraints in an integrated and systematic way. The strategic elements or policies can also be assessed against each other for compatibility purposes.

The HoQ, as its name implies, is a quality management mega tool.[1] It was originally developed in the designing and manufacturing of large oil tankers in Japanese shipyards in the 1970s. It has since been linked with Six Sigma Quality and also to construction sustainability in my previous book. However, the HoQ is also a surprisingly robust approach to developing a strategy, and despite the reputation of being the most complex of all quality management tools, it is actually quite simple to use. It is not necessarily easy, but it is very practical, so two out of three is not bad.

Having introduced the concept of HoQ to you, I need to come clean to say that there isn't a definitive version of the HoQ (gulp!), but there are versions that are generally more difficult to deploy than others. The model is made up of multiple matrices, up to 25 in some cases. The version I am proposing to you below runs with (only) seven matrices, as it is sufficient to develop strategy, policy and management activities. By the way, the House part of the HoQ comes from the roof-shaped Correlations Matrix at the top, as shown on Figure A3.1. These steps are described below in sequence. Figure A3.1 shows a stylised description of the HoQ.

The Needs Matrix

This is the requirement the organisation need to fulfil. This is probably the main reason your organisation is in existence. However, as the world evolves and changes, the needs may also evolve and you need to keep these updated.

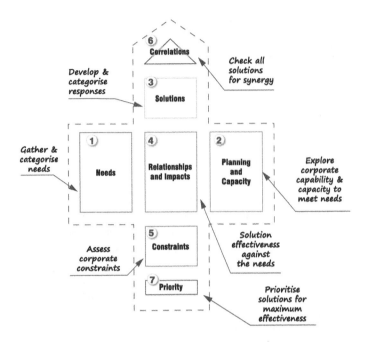

Figure A3.1 The House of Quality.

A simple starting point in determining the needs is to use corporate business frameworks to create needs categories. For example:

- PEST analysis: What are the Political/Economic/Social/Technological needs?
- Balanced Scorecard: What are the Customer/Finance/Processes/Staff needs?
- Triple Bottom Line: What are the Profit People/Planet needs?

The reason for selecting these models is because they offer a complete framework, and you will not miss out on a critical area if you start with them. By grouping various needs into similar strands, it may be possible to combine these into a compromise need. However, do remember customers do not always like compromised needs – they want what *THEY* want.

At this stage, the needs are generally quite high-level needs, and once a list of needs is compiled, you can further categorise them by their importance to your organisation. I recommend something simple like a five-point scale with 1 for low and 5 for high – it doesn't matter what scale you choose to rank as long as you are consistent in your usage.

The Needs Matrix lists the "Whats" in the What/How Matrix described in Chapter 4.

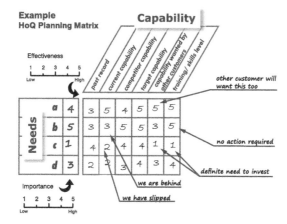

Figure A3.2 HoQ Planning Matrix – Example.

The Planning and Capacity Matrix

This is your organisation's capabilities and capacity in delivering the needs. This matrix can become unwieldy if there are too many elements, but essentially you need to ask: Do we have the skills/capacity/resources to deliver the goods? What was our performance when we deliver this type of outcomes previously? Do we know how our competitors are doing in these areas? Also, if we develop this capacity, will other customers want it? This matrix is shown in Figure A3.2.

The information in this matrix feeds two other matrices: the Solutions Matrix in that your capabilities and capacity determine the type of solutions you can offer and the Constraints Matrix checks whether they are going to be easy or difficult to implement.

The Solutions Matrix

This is a list of the solutions[2] that can deliver the needs. These can be policy elements in a strategy, activities to fulfil the strategy or activities to enable fulfilling the strategy. Again, grouping them under various categories can clarify matters. This matrix correlates the Hows to the Whats from the Needs Matrix. At this stage, the solutions are options that may have varying capabilities to fulfil the needs.

The Relationships and Impacts Matrix

This is the manifestation of the What/How Matrix and the most complicated part of the HoQ to describe. The complexity comes in that this matrix is a multiple-relations matrix where each solution parameter is checked for its effectiveness in delivering against one or more needs. This is shown in Figure A3.3.

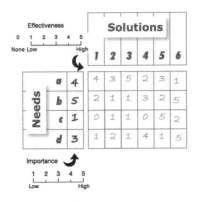

Figure A3.3 HoQ Relationships and Impacts Matrix – Example.

Notice the "importance" column on the Needs Matrix, as described in a previous paragraph; this allows you to rank the importance of the particular needs and can also act as the weighting factor for that particular need.

In Figure A3.4, the right diagram shows the impacts recalculated with a weighting factor. A subtotal score for each solution gives an indication of the relative effectiveness of each solution against the list of needs.

In the left example, Solution 6 is the most effective choice followed by Solutions 5 and 4 in order.

With the weighting factor applied, Solution 6 still has the highest impact against the list of needs, but Solution 4 offers a higher overall impact against the needs when compared with Solution 5.

In reality, it is likely that both Solutions 6 and 5 will be chosen, as they offer the best combined coverage for all the needs. If the budget is sufficient, then Solution 3 may also be selected to cover Need A.

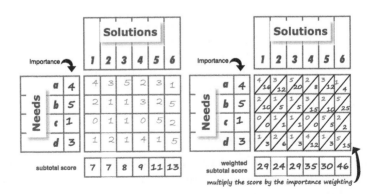

Figure A3.4 Relationships and Impacts Matrix.

Example

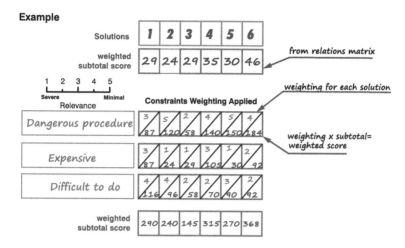

Figure A3.5 Constraints Matrix – with Weightings Applied.

The Constraints Matrix

The Constraints Matrix is the first reality check following the listing of possible solutions and how effective they appear in delivering the needs. The Constraints are things that the organisation may find difficult to achieve and this will hamper the way the delivery is achieved. For these factors to be weighted properly, it is necessary to swap the weighting scale such that severe impacts score 1 and minimal impacts score 5. Figure A3.5 shows the continuing example and how the Constraints Matrix affects the subtotal scores.

You may wish to select more factors that may impact the strategy elements, and perhaps a different set for the implementation activities. The choice really depends on your organisation's capabilities and capacity as outlined in the Planning Matrix.

The Correlations Matrix

Now, we have a list of policy elements or activities assessed for their effectiveness in delivering the required needs. We have further checked these solutions against corporate constraints. Now we get to the second reality check – will they work together? This is where the Correlations Matrix comes in.

Initially, this matrix looks somewhat formidable and a bit incomprehensible (Figure 9.16). But the objective is quite straightforward – to show how the various solutions interact with each other. This matrix uses a 0–5 scale for compatibility, and solutions that are not effective are not considered.

Now, Figure A3.6 looks pretty impressive and most people will just stare at it and think "?". However, this matrix is really a bit of "jargon in a visual context." Whoever invented it was probably so pleased with the metaphor of a House/Roof such that function is sacrificed in favour of form! When you look at Figure A3.7, you will see that it is merely half a square matrix and turned on its side. The analysis is suddenly much easier as we are visually more familiar with this context.

My suggestion is that you carry out the analysis with the old-fashioned square matrix but present your results in the "Roof" format and show off! (And why not?)

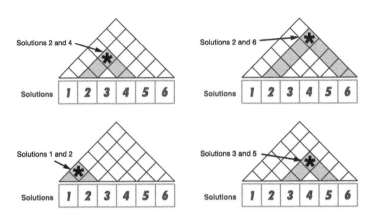

Figure A3.6 Correlations Matrix – Examples.

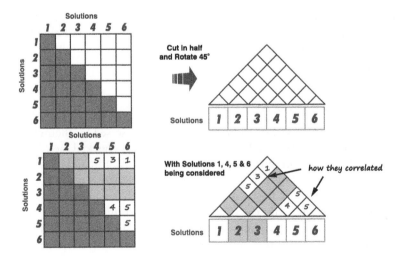

Figure A3.7 The "Easier" Correlations Matrix.

Prioritisation Matrix

This is a very straightforward matrix because you need to look at the highest scoring solutions that cover your needs. Since it has been through the Constraints and Correlations Matrices, you will know that these solutions offer the most efficient and effective way forward (Figure A3.8).

However, the HoQ analysis is based on the initial data, and if circumstances changed since, you will need to take these into account with perhaps different solutions or different phrasing.

Implementing the Prioritisation Matrix will also require a quick check with the Needs Matrix to check the original needs and see whether these are still valid and to check that the solutions do address to the needs.

And there you have it, using the HoQ to design a coherent and integrated strategy or a set of activities to fulfil the strategy. It wasn't so bad now, was it?

Of course, you may wish to use the HoQ to explore further lower level activities. That is entirely possible, but it is also where the "fun" can start.

Quality Function Deployment or HoQ on Steroids

So far, the HoQ model is logical and straightforward, but it also can quickly show its mad side, and this is often known as the Quality Function Deployment (QFD). Each set of solutions (the Hows) readily becomes the next set of needs (the Whats). This cascade starts very logically as it helps you break down the main solution elements. Therefore, the first cascade lets you develop ways to fulfil the strategic elements, and the second cascade gets you into the details of the implementations (See Figure A3.9).

So far so good, but what happens when you want to find out the full details about time taken or the resources deployed? Figure A3.9 shows how a

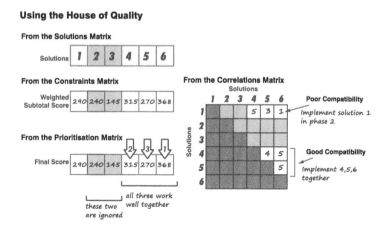

Figure A3.8 From Solution to Priorities – Example.

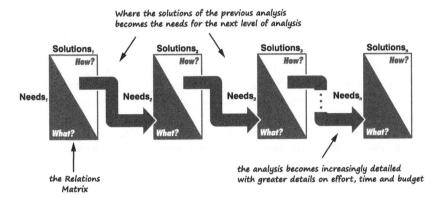

Figure A3.9 Cascading HoQ – The Quality Function Deployment.

QFD can develop from cascading HoQs. The cascade can go on and on until you find out that to fulfil the corporate strategy on sustainability, you need to brush your teeth in the morning and that takes two minutes... Sorry, I joke, but you can see that as the details come out the tool becomes more and more unmanageable. You will eventually get to the costs of individual paper clips and standard times to recalculate a spreadsheet, but this way leads to madness! Although highly detailed, it is no longer easy, simple or practical, except for very simple projects.

For me, this actually adds to the appeal of the HoQ, as this is a technique that does not suffer fools and comes with a (mental) health warning: Know your scope before you start, or you will need a very, very large piece of paper.

Notes

1 Mega tool is quality jargon for a tool framework, but I can't resist using it, as it is such wonderful jargon.
2 I also called these "options" in Chapter 7, but formally in HoQ jargon, these are called Substitute Quality Characteristics. I can explain this interesting fact but it will probably take another chapter and my publisher will then think I am padding this book ...

Index

For Product Safety Concerns and Information please contact our EU
representative GPSR@taylorandfrancis.com Taylor & Francis Verlag GmbH,
Kaufingerstraße 24, 80331 München, Germany

Printed and bound by CPI Group (UK) Ltd, Croydon, CR0 4YY
08/05/2025
01864409-0001